DTN

A Rai

A Raisin in the Sun

Lorraine Hansberry

Methuen

Methuen

1 3 5 7 9 10 8 6 4 2

First published in the United States of America in 1959
First published in Great Britain in 2001 by Methuen Publishing Limited

This complete edition published in 2001 by Methuen Publishing Limited
215 Vauxhall Bridge Road, London SW1V 1EJ

The excerpt from Langston Hughes' poem 'Montage of a Dream Deferred' was
first published in 1951 by Henry Holt & Co. It is reprinted here by permission of
Harold Ober Associates Incorporated.

Copyright © Lorraine Hansberry Estate 1959

Methuen Publishing Limited Reg. No. 3543167

A CIP catalogue record for this book is available from the British Library

ISBN 0 413 76240 8

Typeset by SX Composing DTP, Rayleigh, Essex
Printed and bound in Great Britain by
Cox & Wyman Ltd, Reading, Berkshire

A Young Vic Theatre Company/Salisbury Playhouse co-production

A RAISIN IN THE SUN

by Lorraine Hansberry

Cast in order of appearance

Ruth Younger	**Cecilia Noble**
Travis Younger	**Daniel Anthony** or
	Adrian Fergus Fuller or
	Dwayne Thomas
Walter Lee Younger	**Lennie James**
Beneatha Younger	**Kananu Kirimi**
Lena Younger	**Novella Nelson**
Joseph Asagai	**Ofo Uhiara**
George Murchison	**Faz Singhateh**
Karl Lindner	**William Chubb**
Bobo	**Faz Singhateh**

Direction **David Lan**
Design **Francis O'Connor**
Lighting **Tim Mitchell**
Sound **Crispian Covell**
Casting **Julia Horan**
Voice & Dialect Coach **Jeannette Nelson**
Dance Consultant **Jeanefer Jean-Charles**
Music Consultants **Richard Hammarton** &
       Mia Soteriou
Projection **Philip Gladwell**

Assistant Director **Afia Nkrumah**
Production Manager (Young Vic) **Paul Russell**
Production Manager (Salisbury) **Chris Bagust**
Company Stage Manager **Jules Michaels**
Deputy Stage Manager **Clare Norwood**
Stage Manager (Salisbury) **Helen Reynolds**
Assistant Stage Manager (Salisbury)
       Georgina Richards
Set and costumes by
Salisbury Playhouse workshops

Place: Southside Chicago
Time: The 1950s

There will be one interval

First performed at Salisbury Playhouse on 11 May 2001
First performed at the Young Vic on 1 June 2001

PLEASE ENSURE THAT ALL MOBILE TELEPHONES, PAGERS AND WATCH ALARMS ARE
SWITCHED OFF BEFORE ENTERING THE AUDITORIUM

A RAISIN IN THE SUN

At the end of the Fifties, a young African American playwright, burst on to the American and world stage with the force of a meteor.

Lorraine Hansberry, to whom the term "young, gifted and Black " was first applied, articulated the hopes and the fears of an American family with the force, precision and compassion of Arthur Miller and Eugene O' Neill. But Hansberry had taken the theatre much farther than them. For hers was a Black family.

It is difficult today to imagine a time when Black people were either brought onstage for comic relief, or were types: The Nurturer, The Tragic Mulatto, The Best Friend. The answer to the great comedian Lennie Bruce's question: "Onstage, what's the difference between Lassie and a Black man? At the end, Lassie lives", was the order of the day.

In 'Raisin', Hansberry dares to say that Black people have inner lives, too, and that we are a part of the great human continuum.

In "Mama", she paints a matriarch whose first obligation is the survival of her family. "Mama" knows that this is both the greatest challenge and the sweetest revenge. Staying alive is revenge against those who had set out to destroy her and her kind. Her every waking moment (and I'm sure her dreams, too) are focussed on that legacy handed down from woman to woman, that every Black woman in the Diaspora is given as her birthright.

"Mama" is both hero and a kind of villain. She has no room in her life for subtlety. She is unable to accommodate the variations on a theme that is post World War Two Black urban life . The realities and aspirations of her children, her daughter-in-law and her grandson are foreign to her.

A new day is coming, one that will soon overtake her and pass her by.

"Walter", Mama's son, must forge out his manhood in the face of not only his formidable mother, but his dead father, his own son, and the society which seeks to constantly emasculate him. His choices, foolish and reckless though they may seem, stem from his need to say "I am!! Deal with this!!"

"Ruth", the wife, is the inheritor of her own mother's warrior spirit, but she is also the Black woman who pleads: "Can't I just have a life? Can't I be left in peace?"

But it is "Beneatha", the younger sister of Walter, and Mama's baby, who is Hansberry's most prescient creation. She foreshadows both the Black Power Movement and Black Pride. Beneatha is a young woman who has come to her own conclusions. She looks to Africa, to the origin of all of us in the African Diaspora as well as the home of humankind. For her, Africa is a beacon and a guide.

Like all great works of art, "Raisin" seems as if it has been with us forever. It may seem dated, but this is because it is so much a part of our culture. Every Black playwright, wherever in the world she or he is , has or is writing a variation of "A Raisin In The Sun." It is the foundation. We cannot imagine the world before it.

Come to *A Raisin In The Sun* as you would to any classic. It speaks to us today as it did almost half a century ago.

It is one of the best examples of the poet Ezra Pound's axiom: "Art is the news that stays new."

Bonnie Greer

THOUGHTS ON *A RAISIN IN THE SUN*

A Raisin in the Sun was a revelation for me.

Today everybody and their mother are talking about 'Afrocentricity'. But Hansberry was writing about it long before it became fashionable. ("Hell no, don't call me no African! I'm a Negro, I'm colored, etc, etc." We've all heard that numerous times.) For me, the brilliance of *Raisin* is the examination of the African American family. And we all have to ask ourselves, have things gotten any better than when the play was written? I have to say I think they've gotten worse.

Like all great works of art, this stuff doesn't get old. And for me *Raisin* is still fresh, it's still relevant. Lorraine Hansberry was a visionary.

Spike Lee

LORRAINE HANSBERRY
1930-1964

Born in 1930 in Southside Chicago, Lorraine Hansberry was brought up in an educated middle-class family. Her father was a successful real-estate broker and her uncle a Harvard professor of African history. When she was eight, the Hansberrys moved to a neighbourhood set aside for white residents. The move violated Chicago Covenant law and the family suffered abuse and repeated attacks on their home before officially being asked to leave. With the help of the National Association for the Advancement of Coloured People, Hansberry's father fought and won an anti-segregation case at the Illinois Supreme Court, which ruled that the Covenant legislation was unconstitutional and should be abolished.

Although her parents could afford to pay for a private education, Lorraine was sent to public schools in protest against social segregation. After graduating, she studied art at the University of Wisconsin before moving to New York hoping for success as a writer. There she divided her time between further study at the Jefferson School for Social Sciences, work as a waitress and cashier and contributing many articles to journals and newspapers including Paul Robeson's *Freedom* Magazine.

In 1953 she married Robert Nemiroff, a white Jewish artist and political activist. In the following years she wrote her first play *A Raisin in the Sun* which was opened in March 1959.

She had made history as the first Black female author to have a work staged on Broadway. The play was a great critical and popular success, making history again when Hansberry became the first Black playwright, the fifth woman and the youngest ever American to win the New York Critics Circle Award. Two years later a film version, starring Sidney Poitier, won a special award at the Cannes Film Festival and Hansberry's screenplay was nominated for a Screen Writers Guild award.

Her second staged play *The Sign in Sidney Brustein's Window* closed on the day Hansberry died of cancer at the age of just 34. She left behind a number of unfinished works including a sketch for an opera, *Toussaint*, and a further play, *Les Blancs*, which Nemiroff completed and produced in 1970. Three years later, Nemiroff and Charlotte Zaltzberg adapted *A Raisin in the Sun* into a Tony Award winning musical, *Raisin*. Nemiroff also compiled fragments of Hansberry's writings under the title *To Be Young Gifted and Black*. This achieved international success when staged at the New York Public Theatre in 1971.

Daniel Anthony *Travis Younger*
Theatre includes *The Lion King*, *Hey Mr Producer* (The Lyceum), *Oliver* (The London Palladium). Television includes *Casualty*, *Native* (BBC). Radio includes *Barrel Boy*, *Mami, Papi, Mial & Me* (BBC Radio 4). Other work includes *Into the Millennium* (Corporate Video for the BBC).

William Chubb *Karl Lindner*
Recent theatre includes *He Stumbled* (Wrestling School). Recent television includes *A & E III* (Granada), *Relic Hunter* (Fireworks). Films include *Milk*, *The Affair of the Necklace* (to be released), *Mrs Caldicot's Cabbage War* (to be released).

Adrian Fergus-Fuller *Travis Younger*
Theatre includes *Whistle Down the Wind* (Aldwych Theatre). Television includes *Grange Hill* (BBC), *SMTV* (LWT). Films include *Secret Laughter of Women*.

Lennie James *Walter Lee Younger*
Theatre includes *This is a Chair* (Royal Court), *Two Gentlemen of Verona* (Globe/New Victory Theatre, New York), *Macbeth*, *The Piano Lesson* (Tricycle Theatre), *The Coup* (Royal National Theatre). Television includes *Storm Damage*, *Undercover Heart*, *Out of the Blue* (BBC), *Comics* (Channel 4), *Cold Feet* (Granada). Films include *24 Hour Party People* (dir. Michael Winterbottom), *Lucky Break* (dir. Peter Caulfield), *Snatch* (dir. Guy Ritchie), *Among Giants* (dir. Sam Miller), *The Martins* (dir. Tony Grounds).

Kananu Kirimi *Beneatha Younger*
Theatre includes Miranda in *The Tempest* (The Globe), Juliet in *Romeo & Juliet*, Cinderella in *Cinderella* (Royal Lyceum, Edinburgh). Television includes *Dead* (Alibi Productions for ITV). Films include *Highlander IV: World Without End*.

Novella Nelson *Lena Younger*
Theatre on Broadway includes *Purlie*, *Having Our Say*, *Hello, Dolly!*, *Caesar and Cleopatra*, *The Little Foxes*. Repertory Theatre includes *Widows*, *Camino Real*, *South Pacific*, *The Cider House Rules*, *To Gleam It Around* at theatres such as The Mark Taper Forum, ACT Seattle Rep, Hartford Stage Company and Crossroads Theatre Company. Television, Movies of the Week and mini-series include *Mama Flora's Family*, *The Summer of Ben Tyler*, *Harambee*, *Sex and the City*, *Oz*, *Law & Order: Special Victims Unit*, *New York Undercover*, *100 Center Street*, *One Life to Live*. Films include *A Perfect Murder*, *The Devil's Advocate*, *The Seduction of Joe Tynan*, *Privilege*, *Mercy*, *Manny & Lo*, *The Keeper*.

Cecilia Noble *Ruth Younger*
Theatre includes *The Tempest*, *Philoctetes* (Cheek By Jowl), *The Birthday Party* (Shared Experience), *The Recruiting Officer* (Royal National Theatre), *Blues for Mister Charlie* (Manchester Royal Exchange), *Amen Corner* (Bristol Old Vic), *Sacred Heart* (Royal Court), *Water, Wine in the Wilderness* (Tricycle Theatre). Television includes *Thieftakers* (Carlton), *Storm Damage* (Screen One), *The Rover*, *Holby City* (BBC), *Space Precinct*. Films include *The Native*, *New Year's Day* (to be released), *Mrs Caldicott's Cabbage War* (to be released).

Faz Singhateh *George Murchison/Bobo*
Theatre includes *Othello* (ReAct Theatre Company), *Twelfth Night* (Salisbury Playhouse and tour of China), *Tickets and Ties* (Theatre Royal Stratford East and tour of Sweden), *My Native Land* (Lyric Hammersmith), *Giant Steps* (Oval House), *A Midsummer Night's Dream*, *Antony & Cleopatra*, *Oroonoko* (Royal Shakespeare Company), *Twelfth Night*, *Hamlet* (Birmingham Rep on tour). Television includes *The Detectives*, *The Bill*, *Between The Lines*, *Oasis*. Films include *The Darkening*.

Dwayne Thomas *Travis Younger*
Television includes *Storm Damage*, *Grange Hill*, *Casualty* (BBC), *The Bill* (Thames), *Watch Your Own Wednesday* (Nickelodeon). Radio includes *Gemeriqui* (BBC). Other credits include a commercial for and presenter of *Nickelodeon* (Nickelodeon).

Ofo Uhiara *Joseph Asagai*
This is Ofo's professional stage debut. Television includes *The Bill* (ITV). Film includes *Lucky Break* (Fragile Films, Film Four).

David Lan *Direction*
Born in Cape Town where he trained as an actor, he came to England in 1972. Productions include *Pericles* (RNT Studio), *The Glass Menagerie* (Watford), *'Tis Pity She's a Whore* and *Julius Caesar* (both Young Vic). For the BBC 'Omnibus' series he directed *Artist Unknown* (1995) and *Royal Court Diaries* (1996). His many plays, screenplays,

adaptations and opera libretti have been produced by the Royal Court, the Almeida, the Royal National Theatre, the Royal Shakespeare Company, BBC TV and Channel Four. He is Artistic Director of the Young Vic Theatre Company.

Francis O'Connor *Design*
Theatre includes *The Beauty Queen of Leenane*, *The Leenane Trilogy* (Druid Theatre/Royal Court & Broadway), *Sacred Heart* (Royal Court), *Peer Gynt* (Royal National Theatre), *Closer* (RNT Touring), *Tarry Flynn*, *Big Maggie*, *Iphigenia at Aulis*, *The Wake*, *The House*, *The Freedom of the City*, *The Colleen Bawn* (Abbey Theatre, Dublin), *Mr Peters Connections* (Signature, New York), *A Small Family Business* (Chichester Festival Theatre), *Honk* (Habimah, Tel Aviv), *La Cava* (Piccadilly Theatre).

Tim Mitchell *Lighting*
Tim's credits include *Noises Off*, (Royal National Theatre/Piccadilly Theatre), *Edward II* (Sheffield Crucible), *Merrily We Roll Along* (Donmar Warehouse), *King John*, *Henry IV Parts I & II*, *Macbeth*, *Jubilee*, *The Lieutenant of Inishmore* (Royal Shakespeare Company), *The Red Balloon*, *The Alchemist* (Royal National Theatre), *Speaking in Tongues* (Derby/Hampstead), *Two Pianos Four Hands* (Comedy Theatre), *Hamlet* (Birmingham Rep), *The Marriage of Figaro*, *Don Giovanni* (Kammeroper Vienna), *Carmen Negra* (Icelandic Opera).

Crispian Covell *Sound*
Trained at Guidhall School of Music and Drama. Sound designs include *Julius Caesar* (Young Vic - London & Tokyo transfer), *The Nativity* (Young Vic - London), *Arabian Nights* (Young Vic UK and International Tour), *The Jewess of Toledo* (Bridewell Theatre), *King Lear*, *Fallen Angels* (Indian Summer Theatre Company – Indian Tour), *Fantastic Mr Fox*, *The Snow Queen* and *Wind in the Willows* (MCN Productions), *Cabaret* (Guildhall Drama School). Other productions include *Noises Off* (Royal National Theatre - UK Tour), *Blood Brothers* (BKL - UK Tour), *Snow White and the Seven Dwarfs* (E&B's No 1 Pantomime, Birmingham & Southampton), *Cirque de Solleil's Alegria* (European Tour), *Kat and the Kings* (European Tour), *Happy Days - The Musical* (E&B Productions - UK Tour), *Swan Lake* (English National Ballet, UK Arena Tour).

Jeanefer Jean-Charles
Dance Consultant
Theatre includes *A Night at the Cotton Club* (Stardust Productions, Holland), *Rent Money* (The Posse), *Jazz Umberella*, *Rhythm Circus*, *Barefeet & Crazy Legs* (Bullies Ballerinas), *Alive Kids* (British Council, South Africa), *The Snow Queen* (Theatre Centre, Warwick Arts Centre), *Moving Voices* (Theatre Centre, National Tour). Television includes *Dancing on the Street* (Channel 4), *Songs of Praise* (BBC). Films include *The Parent Trap* (Walt Disney). Other credits include *Tina Turner in Concert* (Camden Palace, Television & Video), *Matt Bianco* (Video), *Tony Scott* (Video), *British Ski Ballet -1992 Olympic Games* (British Olympic Association).

Jeannette Nelson *Voice and Dialect Coach*
Jeanette has worked as Voice Coach at the Royal National Theatre since 1992. She has also worked at Shakespeare's Globe and the Guildhall School of Music and Drama. Theatre credits include *Credible Witness* (Royal Court), *Merrily We Roll Along* (Donmar Warehouse), *The Graduate* (Gielgud Theatre), *The King & I* (London Palladium), *Mama Mia* (Prince Edward Theatre). Television work includes *Great Expectations*, *All The Kings Men*, *Nature Boy*, *David Copperfield*, *The Sins*, *The Mayor of Casterbridge*, *Love in a Cold Climate* (all BBC).

Afia Nkrumah *Assistant Director*
Theatre includes *Come and Go* (Nuffield Theatre, Southampton), *The Three Sisters* (British Council tour of East Africa), *Chasing* (Hen & Chickens), *Deux Ex Machina* (Der Norske Theatret, Oslo). Also, as Assistant Director *Home & Garden* (Royal National Theatre – Staff Director).

SALISBURY PLAYHOUSE – CO-PRODUCER

Salisbury Playhouse is a regional producing theatre, serving Salisbury and the wider region of Wiltshire, Hampshire and Dorset. It presents its productions in both its 517 seat main house and its 140 seat studio throughout the year, and also operates a thriving education and outreach department and youth theatre. In December 1996, the Playhouse completed a major refurbishment programme, made possible by a grant of £1.47 million from the National Lottery, through the Arts Council of England. In summer 1998, the Playhouse was also awarded £281,000 for a programme of artistic and audience development through the Arts for Everyone Scheme, funded by the National Lottery.

In 1998, Salisbury Playhouse was one of three theatres in the country nominated for the new and prestigious Barclays Award for Theatre of the Year. The programme of work in the Salberg Studio was also recognised with an award for special regional achievement in the Empty Space... Peter Brook Awards.

The Beauty Queen of Leenane

Since re-opening, in September 1995, the Playhouse has developed its reputation both regionally and nationally with a broad-ranging and high quality programme of work. Recent highlights have included a provocative revival of David Hare's *The Secret Rapture*, an innovative staging of Martin McDonagh's *The Beauty Queen of Leenane* in the Salberg Studio, a highly-acclaimed production of Peter Shaffer's *Equus* (for which the 517 seat main house was transformed into the round) and the Springboard project, now in its second year (a mini-rep. season for new drama school graduates to gain their first professional stage experience).

The Circle

Co-productions and collaborations have become an increasing part of the Playhouse's work over the last few years and co-production partners have included Oxford Stage Company (W. Somerset Maugham's *The Circle*), Shared Experience Theatre (Lorca's *The House of Bernarda Alba*) and Coventry Belgrade and Watford Palace (Brian Friel's *Translations*). Salisbury Playhouse is delighted to be collaborating with the Young Vic on this production.

COMING SOON AT SALISBURY PLAYHOUSE

Thursday 14 June - Saturday 7 July
SECOND FROM LAST IN THE SACK RACE
by Michael Birch from the novel by David Nobbs
directed by Douglas Rintoul
designed by Su Houser
lighting designed by Peter Hunter

"There's nowt so queer as folk" said the parrot!

And that is so true in the experience of our hero Henry Pratt. "Pratt by name, prat by nature" many would say, but there is more to our Henry than meets the eye. Born in a back–to–back house in 1935 Henry seems to be saddled with a few stumbling blocks, hindering him from making the most of his life and there's a war on. But fate twists and turns for Henry, taking him into unexpected situations, until he finally does seem to be making it up the social ladder.

This is a fast-paced and witty comedy. Wry and entertaining, *Second from Last in the Sack Race* has a northern bite that will have you in stitches. With punchy one-liners and shades of poignancy, Michael Birch has masterfully blended David Nobbs' narrative style with a lively dialogue.

Director's Masterclass	Tuesday 22 June
Post Show Talkout	Tuesday 3 July
Theatre Day	Thursday 5 July

Thursday 6 September - Saturday 29 September
THE RIVALS
by Richard Brinsley Sheridan
directed by Tim Luscombe
designed by Nancy Surman
lighting designed by Peter Hunter

Adversaries duel… ladies languish… and all for love

This is a very funny and delightful classic comedy set in Regency Bath. From the writer of many restoration comedies, including *A School for Scandal* comes this, one of his most humorous and stylish plays.

Captain Absolute, heir to a tidy fortune, loves Lydia Languish, but she, being a principled woman will not marry anyone unless they too despise money. Captain Absolute has a cunning plan to win over Lydia but he finds there is a rival to his lady's love. With various characters concealing their true appearances, we see countless cases of mistaken identity with comic consequences. At the heart of the play sits Mrs Malaprop, one of the most wonderful comic characters that has ever graced the stage.

Post Show Talkout	Tuesday 25 September
Theatre Day	Thursday 27 September

Sponsored by

PLAYHOUSE PATRONS

Formed in 1991, The Salisbury Playhouse Friends and Patrons organisation now has over 1,000 members whose subscriptions, donations and other activities contribute enormously to the running of the theatre. Friends and Patrons come from all walks of life, but all have one thing in common - an enthusiasm for the theatre, in general and Salisbury Playhouse, in particular.

Those listed below are current Salisbury Playhouse Patrons. Their generosity is providing a valuable contribution to the running of our theatre.

Life Patrons
Revd. Canon S. Collins
Mrs D Eyers
Mrs J Lemon
Dr & Mrs M E Moore

Mr & Mrs J Ashenden
Lt. Col. J C Avery
Dr & Mrs B Batten
Lady Bessborough
Miss D Bickmore
Dr J A Birch
Dr & Mrs A G Blyth
Miss J Bowen
Mrs S A Bourne
Mrs J. Bradby
Mrs C Bradish
Mr & Mrs F Brenan
Sqdn. Ldr. D J Chapman
Mrs E O Cooke
Mrs E M Cornelius Reid
Mr & Mrs G Crawley
Mrs P Crossland
Mr & Mrs Ashley Deacon
Mrs K M Dent
Dr & Mrs J M English
Mrs J M Eversfield
Mr & Mrs C J Gradidge
Mr & Mrs John Gradwell
Mr John Green
Mrs R C Griffen
Dr & Mrs B M Guyer
Mr and Mrs P W Halliden
Mr & Mrs D Hitchings
Mr & Mrs G R Hodge
Mrs S Howard Smith
Mr R Humphry
Dr & Mrs B W Hunt
Mr & Mrs B J Hurst Bannister

Revd M Hurst Bannister
Mrs P Hurst Bannister
Rev & Mrs J Izzard
Mr D J Jackson
Mrs Margot Jessop
Mr & Mrs N Johnston
Mrs D Keatinge
Mrs R A Lamb
Barbara Lawton
Mr & Mrs H Letty
Mrs M M Lemon
Brigadier & Mrs D R H Longfield
Mrs J A Longley
Commander J Loring
Mr & Mrs C H Love
Mrs Beryl V Lush
Ms Catherine MacRae
Mr W J Q Magrath
Mrs D Main
Mr B Mair
Mrs J Markham
Mr & Mrs J Marland
Mr & Mrs C G Martin
Mr & Mrs N V Martin
Mrs T W Martin
Mr & Mrs P Martineau
Lt Col & Mrs R M S Maude
Ms J McClement
Ms Rosaleen Moyne
Miss M B Nairn
Mr & Mrs P D Newman
Mrs O R Nicholas
Mr C J Oliver
Mr Graham Osgood
Mr & Mrs R W B Patterson
Mrs M Pattle
Mr M S Pearce
Sir John and Lady Peel

Mrs J Peto
Sir Haden & Hon Lady Phillips
Mr & Mrs J A M Pitcairn
Mrs C Pope
Mrs J P Porkess
Mr K Porter
Mr H C Quitman
Mr J.C. Ryder Richardson
Col & Mrs B F L Rooney
Mrs S Rutt
Mr & Mrs A C B Schomberg
Mr & Mrs D Sealey
Mr & Mrs T M Sims
Mr & Mrs C J Slater
Mr M Slater
Mr & Mrs R W Sloley
Mrs M Smale
Mr & Mrs D Stephenson
Mrs Veronica Stewart
Mr T C Stevens
Mr & Mrs J C Stoller
Rev R F Swan
Dr F G Tait
Mr E S Teversham
Mr & Mrs N C E Tongue
Mrs B J Turner
Mr and Mrs Robert Vincent
Mr George Wakley
Miss S M Ward
Mr M Warrander
Mr & Mrs I G Watson
Mr & Mrs J Whatley
Mrs A Wheatley Hubbard
Miss P J Whitehead
Mr & Mrs A G Witt
Mr & Mrs D J Wood
Mrs E M Wootton

SALISBURY PLAYHOUSE GROUP PATRONS

Dorset Theatregoers Club (Weymouth)
Dorset Theatregoers Club (Purbeck Area)
Dorset Theatregoers Club (Bournemouth)

SPONSORSHIP AND CORPORATE SUPPORT

MARKETING, ENTERTAINING, CONTRIBUTING

Whether you are seeking to promote your business, entertain your clients and reward staff, or simply wanting to contribute to this community resource, the Playhouse can tailor a package of benefits to meet YOUR commercial objectives. Support from successful companies enables the Playhouse to deliver nationally renowned theatre to an audience of more than 100,000 annually, as well as educational work for schools in Wiltshire, Hampshire and Dorset, and we are very grateful to the following for their valued support this season. For further information about sponsorship and corporate support please call Rebecca Morland on 01722 320117.

PRODUCTION SPONSORS

for their sponsorship of *The Miser*

for their sponsorship of the Summer Season 2001 in the Salberg Studio

CORPORATE PATRONS

Avon Advertiser/Salisbury Journal
Chas H. Baker
Beechcroft Classic Country Homes
Charade Dry Cleaners
Friends Provident
Gerrard
HSBC
Hollyhock
Howard's House County Hotel and
Restaurant
Le Hérisson Brasserie and Delicatessen
Myddleton and Major
Nadder Food and Events
Nat West
I. N. Newman Funeral Directors
Personal Pension Management
The Red Lion Hotel, Salisbury
Sarum Cleaning Services
WHSmith
The Smith and Williamson Group
SMS Office Equipment
Limited/Computers dot.com
Trethowan's Solicitors
Margaret Turner Fine Jewellery
Wessex Electricals/Wessex Fire and
Security
Wetherby Moore Training Ltd.
Whitehead Vizard Solicitors

CORPORATE ASSOCIATES

Allum and Sidaway Ltd.
Dinghams
Fieldfare Properties Ltd.
Jolly Property Services
S. Moody Company. (Salisbury Ltd.)
Pennyfarthings Property Management
Plastic Technology Service Ltd.
Rawlence and Brown Ltd.
Old George Mall

SALISBURY PLAYHOUSE EDUCATION & OUTREACH

education@salisburyplayhouse.com

Each season, the Playhouse Education Department offers a wide and varied selection of both Educational and Creative Workshops, Theatre Days, Talkouts, Children's shows and Theatre Experiences for all ages.

Workshops

For schools, colleges, community groups and young people we have a range of in-house and at your venue workshops based on our current productions that can enhance curriculum work, theatre studies and creative skills.

Switched On Theatre Experiences for Children

A joint programme with Salisbury Arts Centre of workshops and theatre experiences for the under 13s and their families. Saturday programme of workshops, puppet shows, storytelling, dance, magic and all-sorts to tickle the funny bones, inspire, intrigue and entertain imaginative minds.

Theatre Days

Theatre Days are an opportunity for everyone interested in the production process to meet the company, both actors and technicians, experience first-hand 'behind-the-scenes' activity and gain a new perspective of moments within the play. These days are followed by a performance of the studied show and a short after show discussion*. To book, please call the Box Office on 01722 320333

Theatre Tours

Backstage tours of the theatre are available to book for groups and school parties priced at £2.50 per adult and £1.50 per student*. Please call the Education Department on 01722 320117 to book.

*prices correct at time of going to press, please check for current rates

PYPA

The Playhouse's Young Persons Association For schools, colleges and young people's organisations.

Membership entitles you to discount on tickets for Main House productions and selected Salberg Studio performances and discounts on selected workshops. For information or to join please call the Box Office on 01722 320333.

Talkout Evenings

Talkout Evenings are free to anyone. These informal discussions with members of the company and cast take place after performances on the last Tuesday of every run for Main House shows.

*subject to show running times.

For more information on any of the above contact the Education & Outreach Officer on 01722 320117.

Macbeth CD-Rom Resource Pack

In HTML format with menu and easy navigation. This resource contains in-depth information about Shakespeare, the Play, Themes, Sources, Interviews, Weblinks, Witchcraft in Macbeth, Photos and Pictures, Production notes from the Director, Lighting Designer and members of the company of the Salisbury Playhouse production (March 2001) plus much more. The CD-Rom costs £10 inclusive of p+p. To obtain your copy call the education department on 01722 422182 or e-mail your order to education@salisburyplayhouse.com.

STAGE '65 YOUTH THEATRE

Stage '65 is Salisbury Playhouse's Youth Theare for anyone aged 11-25. Weekly drama sessions are offered in theatre skills both for performers and for those interested in the technical side of theatre. Members have the opportunity to perform regularly as well as receiving saver deals for Playhouse productions. Recent and future work includes a lavish stage adaptation of Charles Dickens' *A Tale of Two Cities* performed in the Main House, a cheeky new musical comedy, *The Rose and the Ring* and *Freefalling*, a week of new writing by members of the group with the guidance of a professional writer.

THEATRE INFORMATION

Artistic Director *Joanna Read*
Executive Director *Rebecca Morland*

RTYDS Director *Douglas Rintoul*

Administration
Theatre Secretary *Sue Edwards*
*Exhibitions Officer *Nancy Strike*

Education & Outreach
Education & Outreach Officer *Juliet Mortimer*

Stage '65 Youth Theatre
Youth Theatre Officer *Caroline Leslie*

Finance
*Finance Manager *Alison Taylor*
Finance Assistant *Caroline Corkill*
*Finance Assistant *Tammy Sibley*

Front of House
Theatre Manager & Licensee *Alan Corkill*

Marketing
Marketing Manager *Fiona Carter*
Marketing Assistant *Kate Smith*
Casting/Marketing Assistant *John Manning*
Box Office Manager *Victoria Rattue*
Deputy Box Office Manager *Suzanne Bell*
*Box Office Assistants *Adrian Cooke*
Amy Cox
Joe Hannington-Smith
Belinda Harding
Darren Little
Karen Morgan
Della Pearce
Kirsty Sully

Production
Production Manager *Chris Bagust*
*Production Assistant *Nicola Davidson*
Lighting Designer/Chief Electrician
Peter Hunter
Deputy Chief Electrician *Paul Stear*
Assistant Electrician *Emma Chapman*
Stage Manager *Helen Reynolds*
Deputy Stage Managers *Chris Westwood*
Julia Reid
Assistant Stage Managers *Jessica Chu*
Georgina Richards
Chief Technician *Suresh Chawla*
Head of Construction *Justin Crofton*
Senior Carpenter *Rhys Gillard*
Scenic Artist *Rod Holt*
Carpenter *Hannah Jenkins*
Wardrobe Supervisor
Henrietta Worrall-Thompson
Deputy Wardrobe Supervisor *Penny Peters*
Wardrobe Assistant *Linda Whitlock*
Dresser *Amy Roberts*
*Hairdressing *Sheila Long*

Togs
Manager *Marion Allen*
*Sales Assistants *Jo Griffin*
Elisabeth Levinson
Jenny Lloyd

Contract Cleaners
Sarum Cleaning Services

Board of Directors
Simon Richards (Chairman)
Ian Gyllenspetz, Laurie Harrington,
Philippa Killner, Desmond Longfield,
Catherine MacRae, Iris Throp (Wiltshire
County Council), Cliff Ware, Jack Wills.

Company Secretary *Rebecca Morland*

The Board of Directors also benefits from the
support of:
Rachel Efemey (Principal Arts & Community
Officer, Salisbury District Council), *Cllr
Donald Culver* (Salisbury District Council),
Nicolas Young (Theatre Officer, Southern
Arts)

Theatre Chaplain *The Rev M Hurst-Bannister*
Theatre Doctor *Dr J A Easton, Harcourt
Medical Centre*
Honorary Archivists *Arthur Millie*
Jane Ware

* denotes part-time

Visiting Creative Team - Summer 2001	Visiting Acting Company - Summer 2001
Richard Beecham	Stephen Billington
Crispian Covell	Jamie Bradley
Richard Foxton	William Chubb
Su Houser	Lisa Ellis
David Lan	Michael Hodgson
Tim Luscombe	Graham Howes
Tim Mitchell	Lennie James
Francis O'Connor	Kananu Kirimi
Nancy Surman	Novella Nelson
	Cecilia Noble
	Maggie Norris
	Brian Poyser
	Shaun Prendergast
	Faz Singhateh
	Ofo Uhiara
	Fenella Woolgar

THEATRE INFORMATION

The Box Office
Salisbury Playhouse
Malthouse Lane
Salisbury SP2 7RA
Tel: 01722 320333

Opening times:
Mon - Sat: 10am - 8pm
(6pm on days when there is
no performance)

Bookings can be made by telephone,
post or in person.
Reservations must be paid for within 7
days.
Please enclose a stamped addressed
envelope otherwise tickets will be held
for collection.

Cheques should be made payable to
Salisbury Playhouse.
Mastercard, Visa, Diners' Club, American
Express and Switch cards are accepted.

Facilities for people with disabilities
We are delighted to welcome people with
disabilities to Salisbury Playhouse.
Please do let us know if you or any of
your party have any special needs when
you make your booking.

Wheelchair users can be accommodated
in two boxes, which are immediately next
to both main doors of the auditorium.
These can be reached easily by the lift in
the Salberg Studio corridor and spaces
need to be booked in advance. Specially
equipped lavatories are also available:
one is near the lift and the other is easily
accessible from the Restaurant.

Guide Dogs (& their owners!) are
welcome.

Infra-red System
The Playhouse has an infra-red system,
which will enable people with hearing
difficulties to enjoy performances in the
Main House. In the future we also plan
to offer audio-described performances for

people who are visually impaired.
Headsets can be booked at the box
office.

This system has been made possible by
fundraising from the Friends & Patrons
Committee of Salisbury Playhouse,
together with a grant from the ADAPT
Trust and the Guide Dogs for the Blind
Association. We are very grateful for
their support.

Volunteers
There are many ways in which you can
help the Playhouse.

If you would like to display our posters or
leaflets then please contact our
Marketing Department on 01722 320117.

Volunteer programme sellers are also
very welcome - if you have a couple of
hours free in the early evening on a
regular basis please contact Alan Corkill,
Theatre Manager, on 01722 320117.

Togs
Fancy Dress Party? School Play? Togs is
the Theatre's own fancy dress hire
service. Please phone 01722 332862 for
further details and for opening times.

RYTDS Director
This theatre is supported by the Richard
Dunn Bursary under The Regional
Theatre Young Director Scheme
administered by Channel Four Television.

Food and Drink
Meet your friends at the Playhouse for
coffee, lunch, afternoon tea or an
evening meal. We are also offering top
quality bar snacks in our foyer.

Playhouse Restaurant
Opens from 9.30am to 5pm, Monday to
Saturday and is also open from 6pm on
performance evenings. Morning coffee,
tasty lunches and afternoon teas are
available throughout the day.

Pre-performance meals range from simple snacks to full three-course meals and our fully-licensed bar means you can wine and dine in style.

Post-performance meals
Enjoy an evening of excellent theatre and then excellent food after the performance.
Advance booking is required for post-performance meals.
For more information or to book a table please call the Box Office on 01722 320333.

Playhouse Bar
Opens from 11am–2.30pm and from 6pm–11pm on performance evenings. A range of bar meals, snacks and drinks are available during the day and before the performance. The Hawkings Bar is available to hire for corporate or private parties. For more information please call Alan Corkill on 01722 320117.

No Smoking Wednesdays
At Salisbury Playhouse, we are aware that some of our patrons do not enjoy the smell of cigarette smoke. To this end we have introduced one evening per week when there will be no smoking in any part of the building after 5.00pm.

Licensing Requirements
1 The audience may leave at the end of the performance by all exit doors.
2 All gangways, corridors, staircases and passages which afford a means of exit shall be kept entirely free from obstruction.
3 Persons shall not be permitted to stand or sit in any of the gangways.

The Salisbury Playhouse gratefully acknowledges the financial support of:

Southern Arts
Salisbury District Council
Wiltshire County Council

Hampshire County Council
Test Valley Borough Council
John Lewis Partnership

The Salisbury Playhouse is a Registered Charity and a Limited Company.
Reg Charity No 249169.
VAT No 188 6842 04.

Phase Two of our development plan, which began with the refurbishment of the Main Auditorium in 1995, was completed in December 1996. Phase Two concentrated on the Front of House areas, including dramatic changes to the foyer, the box office, the bar and the restaurant. The Salberg Studio has also seen the installation of new seating and an audience gallery.

 This work has been supported by: Salisbury District Council and the support of individuals, businesses and trusts through our seat sponsorship scheme.

Salisbury Playhouse - on behalf of Salisbury Arts Centre and Salisbury City Hall - gratefully acknowledges a grant from the National Lottery through the Arts Council of England towards the establishment of a Joint Ticketing Network in Salisbury.

THE YOUNG VIC THEATRE COMPANY

The Young Vic is a theatre for everybody but, above all, for younger artists and a younger audience.

We present seasons of classic plays – old and new – and each year we create theatrical events that embrace young people, children and adults in a single experience.

At the heart of all our work is our auditorium. Its unique, humane proportions express and influence everything we as a company feel and think and do. Built of humdrum materials – breezeblock and steel – it's a machine for the imagination, generating fantasy and debate with equal enthusiasm. No one sits more than 5 rows from the stage. The seats are unreserved; each has a perfect view. It's small enough to house a whole society and just big enough to be filled by a single gesture. It's a theatre for a democracy – a people's theatre for engaged imaginative people who love a good time.

Through accidents of history, many people, especially the young, believe that theatre belongs to "other people" of another class or another generation. But playwrights write for the whole world. So for each of our main house productions we prepare an extensive programme of Teaching, Participation and Research (TPR) aimed at our local schools and colleges. Hundreds of young people accept our invitation to work with our actors and technicians, discovering theatre and how they can be part of it. We offer on-stage production workshops, an annual Schools' Theatre Festival and written resource material. We provide an extensive work-experience and apprenticeship programme for young people and young professionals. All this work is offered free of charge. One of our core ideas is that by teaching others about theatre, we learn.

Our Studio offers many of our younger directors and small-scale companies a chance to experiment. Seating about 80, it has a powerful reputation for daring, innovative productions.

Over 100,000 visit us in London each year. A further 50,000 see our work on national and international tours. We keep our prices low and make a priority of developing new audiences. The Funded Ticket Scheme is a further enducement to people of all ages and backgrounds who might not otherwise visit us to do so. Created in 1994, it reaches into many sectors of Lambeth and Souhwark, our local boroughs. Last year almost 10% of our audience came under this scheme.

How is all this paid for? We are funded by London Arts, the Arts Council of England, London Borough Grants and Lambeth and Southwark Councils. This makes up 26% of our income. The remaining 74% is generated through our box office, through international touring and, by our development department, through sponsorship and donations.

This year we're launching a series of new projects to give young directors the chance to direct major productions in our main house and our studio. Watch this space for details.

We believe that our theatre should be a place of energy, intelligence and pleasure. Join us whenever you can.

SUPPORTING THE YOUNG VIC

Since its earliest days, the Young Vic has counted on the support of many enlightened partners. This commitment to our work has enabled us to establish an unequalled reputation for presenting great plays - classics and new work - in innovative, accessible productions.

To build on this success the Young Vic needs your help.

We are grateful to our public funders – London Arts, London Borough Grants Committee and Lambeth and Southwark Council - for their ongoing contribution to our work. However, public funding and box office income combined provide only 61% of our operating income. The remainder, some £1 million a year, must be raised through sponsorship, trust donations and private contributors in order for us to mount world-class productions, give opportunities to theatre artists of the future and work with young people and the local community.

Our existing theatre was built, to last only five years, in 1970. It is now in a critical state of repair and a constant drain on our scarce resources. Whilst we have plans to redevelop the current facility in the future, there are many pressing needs to ensure the building meets health and safety requirements and allows artists and production teams to have the basic conditions they need to work.

We are tremendously grateful for the wholehearted commitment of our many supporters and sponsors. However, to meet the ongoing challenges of our ambitious artistic programme, extend our outreach work, develop new audiences and maintain the building, **we need your support now more than ever before**.

Please get involved with us by joining as a Young Vic Friend or, if you are able, by making a significant contribution to an area of our work through The Director's Circle. Friends' leaflets may be picked up in the foyer or, for further information and a discussion on The Director's Circle please call Naomi Russell in the Development Office on 020 7633 0133.

We need your support.

YOUNG VIC SUPPORTERS

INDIVIDUAL SUPPORTERS

The Director's Circle
Tony Bloom

Stage Partners
Anonymous
Edwin C Cohen
Val Gilbert
John & Sue Kinder
Jane Lucas
Justin Shinebourne
David & Maria Willetts

Leading Role
Robyn Durie
Miss Nadine Majaro
Terence Pentony

Supporting Cast
Anonymous
Mr C J Bates
Tom Bendhem
Alex & Angela Bernstein
Katie Bradford
Chris Carter
Gillian Diamond
Ruth Downing
Lisa & Gerard Fairtlough
Clare Garvin
Anthony & Jennifer Gubbins
Sue Hammerson
Sheila Harvey
Dr & Mrs Joe Herzberg
Mr & Mrs W Hicks
Philip Hobbs
Mary Hustings
The King's School,
Canterbury
Lady Lever
London Theatre &
Restaurant Club
Victor & Marilyn Lownes
Patrick McKenna
Georgia Oetker
Marco Roggero
Mrs Anthony Salz
Lois Sieff
Dr Martin Smith
Lady Swire
Jan & Michael Topham
The Tracy Family
Rebecca Winnington-Ingram
Paul & Sybella Zisman

Backstage Crew
Mrs A M Allen
Anonymous
Martin Bowley QC
Rob Brooks
Julian Burton
Christina Burton
Allegra Castellini
Rosemary Carawan
Paula Clemett
Martin Cliff
Conway van Gelder
Jessica Fenton
Robert Gardiner
Mr M Graham Smith
Michael Greenhalgh
Richard Hardman
Anya Jones
Christopher Hancock
Lew Hodges
Dr Kingsley Jones
Pamela Lane
Nicholas C Lewis
Paul & Brigitta Lock
Tony & Mary Mackintosh
Mr & Mrs R Marshall
Christopher & Dea Maude
Neil Mundy
Paul Mendelson
Anthea Minnett
Barbara Minto
Nuala Nation
Mr Oliver John Nicholson
Mrs G M C Phillips
Nick Pizey
Cindy Polemis
Barbara, Lady Poole
Richard Price Television
Associates
Liz & Roger Shaw
Mr K H Simmonds
Richard Slater
Ann & Peter Snow
Christine Stevenson
Mr & Mrs David Van Oss
Janet Walker
Anthony Watkinson
George & Patti White
G & E Wickham

And to the Friends of the
Young Vic whose ongoing
support of the theatre is
invaluable

Season Sponsor
Ambassador
Theatre Group Ltd

Production Sponsors & Supporters
The Blessing Way
Foundation
The David Cohen Family
Charitable Trust
The Quercus Trust
The Times
The Tara Ulemek
Foundation

Two Boroughs Project Sponsors
Ingenious Media

Funded Ticket Scheme Sponsors
Allied Domecq
JP Morgan

CORPORATE SUPPORTERS

The Director's Circle
Brunswick

Corporate Donors
3i
Allen & Overy
Arthur Anderson Foundation
Barclays Bank
Barclays Life Assurance
Company
Bass
The Berkeley Group
Bloomberg LP
British Steel
Cubana
Direct Connection
Frogmore Estates
Singer & Friedlander
Limited
The Guardian Royal
Exchange Charitable Trust

IBM (UK) Ltd
ICI
John Lewis Partnership
JP Morgan
London Stock Exchange
London Weekend Television
Manches & Co Solicitors
The Morgan Crucible
Company
News International
Pricewaterhouse Coopers
Railtrack
Royal & Sun Alliance
Sainsbury's
Shell International
Slaughter & May
David S Smith (Holdings)
South West Trains Ltd

Trusts and Foundations
The Ancaster Trust
Anonymous
Ambrose & Ann Appelbe Trust
Avenue Charitable Trust
The E M Behrens
          Charitable Trust
The Worshipful Company o
          Brewers
Carlton Television Trust
The Carnegie United

          Kingdom Trust
City Parochial Foundation
Cliff Richard (Charitable
          Trust) Ltd
Miss V L Clore's 1967
          Charitable Trust
The Muriel & Gershon
    Coren Charitable Trust
The Corporation of London
The D'Oyly Carte Charitable

Trust
The Enid Blyton Trust for
          Children
Foundation for the
          Performing Arts
Forte Charitable Trust
The Grocer's Charity
Mrs Margaret Guido's
          Charitable Trust
The Calouste Gulbenkian
          Foundation
Haberdasher's Eleemsynary
          Charity
JLD Trust
The Ian Karten Charitable Trust
The Mathilda & Terence
    Kennedy Charitable Trust
The Kobler Trust
The Lambert Charitable Trust
The Lynn Foundation
The Mercers' Company
The Milbourn Charitable Trust
The Peter Minet Trust
Lady Neville's Charity
Newcommen Collett
          Foundation
The Persula Foundation
The Austin & Hope
   Pilkington Charitable Trust
George & Esme Pollitzer
          Charitable Settlement
The Albert Reckitt
          Charitable Trust
The Reuter Foundation
The Royal Victoria Hall
          Foundation
Sir Walter St. John's
          Educational Charity
The Scarfe Charitable Trust
Simon's Charity
Thomas Sivewright Catto

          Charitable Settlement
The Snipe Charitable Trust
The Stanley Foundation Ltd
The Star Foundation
St Olave's & St Saviour's
Grammar School Foundation
The Trusthouse Charitable
          Foundation
The Vandervell Foundation
The Roger Waters Charitable
          Trust
The Weinstock Fund
The Garfield Weston
          Foundation
The Whitbread 1988
          Charitable Trust
The Harold Hyam Wingate
          Foundation

Building Campaign
Equity Trust Fund
Patrick McKenna
The National Lottery
through the Arts Council of
England Small-Scale
Capital Programme

**Young Directors
Programmes**
Foundation for Sport and
          the Arts
The Jerwood Foundation
The Mackintosh Foundation

This theatre is supported by
the Mackintosh Foundation
under the Regional Theatre
Young Director Scheme
administered by Channel
Four Television.

The Young Vic receives public funding from

COMING SOON AT THE YOUNG VIC

8 June - 30 June, Studio Theatre
A Young Vic Theatre Company production
STREETCAR TO TENNESSEE
early short plays by Tennessee Williams, directed by Timothy Sheader

7 July - 14 July, Main Theatre & Studio
The Young Vic presents
push
A diverse re-mix of contemporary arts, culture and media
www.pushherenow.com

20 July - 11 August, Studio Theatre
A Young Vic Theatre Company production
ACTION
by Sam Shepard, directed by Arlette Kim George

22 August - 8 September, Main Theatre
The Young Vic presents a Théâtre des Bouffes du Nord production
THE TRAGEDY OF HAMLET
by William Shakespeare, directed by Peter Brook

SEASON SPONSORS - THE AMBASSADOR THEATRE GROUP LTD

The Ambassador Theatre Group (ATG) is renowned for its highly successful management and ownership of theatre venues throughout the country and is currently the second biggest theatre owning group in the West End and, separately, the second biggest in the regions, with a total of 18 buildings.

ATG's impressive portfolio of West End theatres includes high profile and historic venues such as, the Albery, Comedy, Duke of York's, New Ambassadors, Phoenix, Piccadilly, Whitehall and Wyndham's. ATG's regional theatres include The Ambassadors Woking encompassing the New Victoria and Rhoda McGaw Theatres and a multiplex cinema complex; the Theatre Royal, Brighton; the Victoria Concert Hall, Stoke-on-Trent; the Regent Theatre, Stoke-on-Trent; the new theatre in Milton Keynes; the Churchill Theatre in Bromley and Richmond Theatre, London.

ATG has its own acclaimed production arm and is about to co-produce the much celebrated Royal Theatre production of *Mouth to Mouth* starring Lindsay Duncan and Michael Maloney and is currently enjoying outstanding success with a co-production of the National Theatre's *Noises Off* on national tour, due to return to the West End in May 2001, starring Lynn Redgrave, a national tour of *Soul Train* starring Sheila Ferguson and a worldwide tour of *A Servant to Two Masters*. Recent ATG West End productions include the world premiere of *Port Authority*, the new play by Conor McPherson, *Shockheaded Peter*, at the Piccadilly Theatre, the Hull Truck Theatre's production, *Bouncers*, Caryl Churchill's *Far Away*, directed by Stephen Daldry in the West End, a new production of Gilbert and Sullivan's *The Mikado*, the UK tour and West End production of *The Mystery of Charles Dickens* starring Simon Callow, and the post West End tour of *H.M.S. Pinafore*.

Other ATG successes include the co-production of *The Weir* (winner of the 1999 Olivier Award for Best New Play) in the West End and on Broadway, The Royal Court Classics Season at the Duke of Yorks, *Smokey Joe's Café* in the West End, *The Rocky Horror Show* in London, nationally and internationally and the Olivier award-winning *Slava's Snowshow*.

ATG's New Ambassadors Theatre in the West End also presents some of the country's most exciting contemporary artists, which have included a co-production of *Speed-the-Plow* by David Mamet, Ayub Khan-Din's *Last Dance at Dum Dum*, *Krapp's Last Tape* starring John Hurt, the award-winning *Spoonface Steinberg*, the multi-Olivier award-winning *Stones in His Pockets*, and Charlotte Jones' *In Flame*.

ATG is also developing a series of creative alliances, based in theatre, but with the potential to form a bridge between media. These unique initiatives include a new joint venture, Natural Nylon Theatre Company, which will bring actors including Jude Law, Sadie Frost, Ewan McGregor, Sean Pertwee and Jonny Lee Miller to the stage and offer further links into film, plus a new co-production company with Trademark Films, makers of *Shakespeare in Love* and, most recently, a new crossover rights packaging and production enabling joint venture company with Carlton Television. In addition, ATG has also recently formed a new co-producing and commissioning alliance with the acclaimed Young Vic Theatre Company.

A Raisin in the Sun

TO MAMA:

in gratitude for the dream

A Raisin in the Sun was first performed in London at the Adelphi Theatre on 4 August 1959. The cast was as follows:

(in order of appearance)

Ruth Younger	Kim Hamilton
Travis Younger	John Adan
Walter Lee Younger (Brother)	Earle Hyman
Beneatha Younger	Olga James
Lena Younger (Mama)	Juanita Moore
Joseph Asagai	Bari Johnson
George Murchison	Scott Cunningham
Karl Lindner	Meredith Edwards
Bobo	Lionel Ngakane
Moving Men	Keefe West, Donald Hoath

Directed by Lloyd Richards

The action of the play is set in Chicago's Southside, sometime between World War II and the present.

Act One
Scene One. Friday morning
Scene Two. The following morning

Act Two
Scene One. Later, the same day
Scene Two. Friday night, a few weeks later
Scene Three. Moving day, one week later

Act Three
An hour later

What happens to a dream deferred?
Does it dry up
Like a raisin in the sun?
Or fester like a sore—
And then run?
Does it stink like rotten meat?
Like a syrupy sweet?

Maybe it just sags
Like a heavy load.

Or does it explode?

—Langston Hughes

Act One

Scene One

The **Younger** *living-room would be a comfortable and well-ordered room if it were not for a number of indestructible contradictions to this state of being. Its furnishings are typical and undistinguished and their primary feature now is that they have clearly had to accommodate the living of too many people for too many years – and they are tired. Still, we can see that at some time, a time probably no longer remembered by the family (except perhaps for* **Mama***), the furnishings of this room were actually selected with care and love and even hope – and brought to this apartment and arranged with taste and pride.*

That was a long time ago. Now the once loved pattern of the couch upholstery has to fight to show itself from under acres of crocheted doilies and couch covers which have themselves finally come to be more important than the upholstery. And here a table or a chair has been moved to disguise the worn places in the carpet; but the carpet has fought back by showing its weariness, with depressing uniformity, elsewhere on its surface.

Weariness has, in fact, won in this room. Everything has been polished, washed, sat on, used, scrubbed too often. All pretences but living itself have long since vanished from the very atmosphere of this room.

Moreover, a section of this room, for it is not really a room unto itself, though the landlord's lease would make it seem so, slopes backward to provide a small kitchen area, where the family prepares the meals that are eaten in the living-room proper, which must also serve as dining-room. The single window that has been provided for these 'two' rooms is located in this kitchen area. The sole natural light the family may enjoy in the course of a day is only that which fights its way through this little window.

At left, a door leads to a bedroom which is shared by **Mama** *and her daughter,* **Beneatha***. At right, opposite, is a second room (which in the beginning of the life of this apartment was probably a breakfast-room) which serves as a bedroom for* **Walter** *and his wife,* **Ruth***.*

Time: Sometime between World War II and the present.

Place: Chicago's Southside.

At Rise: It is morning dark in the living-room. **Travis** *is asleep on* *the make-down bed at centre. An alarm clock sounds from within the bedroom at right, and presently* **Ruth** *enters from that room and closes the door behind her. She crosses sleepily towards the window. As she passes her sleeping son she reaches down and shakes him a little. At the window she raises the shade and a dusky Southside morning light comes in feebly. She fills a pot with water and puts it on to boil. She calls to the boy, between yawns, in a slightly muffled voice.*

Ruth *is about thirty. We can see that she was a pretty girl, even exceptionally so, but now it is apparent that life has been little that she expected, and disappointment has already begun to hang in her face. In a few years, before thirty-five even, she will be known among her people as a 'settled woman'.*

She crosses to her son and gives him a good, final, rousing shake.

Ruth   Come on now, boy, it's seven thirty! (*Her son sits up at last, in a stupor of sleepiness.*) I say hurry up, Travis! You ain't the only person in the world got to use a bathroom! (*The child, a sturdy, handsome little boy of ten or eleven, drags himself out of bed and almost blindly takes his towels and 'todays clothes' from drawers and a closet and goes out to the bathroom, which is in an outside hall and which is shared by another family or families on the same floor.* **Ruth** *crosses to the bedroom door at right and opens it and calls in to her husband.*) Walter Lee! . . . It's after seven thirty! Lemme see you do some waking up in there now! (*She waits.*) You better get up from there, man! It's after seven thirty I tell you. (*She waits again.*) All right, you just go ahead and lay there and next thing you know Travis be finished and Mr. Johnson'll be in there and you'll be fussing and cussing round here like a mad man! And be late too! (*She waits, at the end of her patience.*) *Walter Lee* – It's time for you to get up!

She waits another second and then starts to go into the bedroom, but is apparently satisfied that her husband has begun to get up. She stops, pulls the door to, and returns to the kitchen area. She wipes her face with a moist cloth and runs her fingers through her sleep-dishevelled hair in a vain effort and ties an apron around her housecoat. The bedroom door at right opens and her husband stands in the doorway in his pyjamas, which are rumpled and mismatched. He is a lean, intense young man in his middle thirties, inclined to quick nervous movements and erratic speech habits and always in his voice there is a quality of indictment.

Walter   Is he out yet?

Ruth   What you meant *out*? He ain't hardly got in there good yet.

Walter (*wandering in, still more oriented to sleep than to a new day*) Well, what was you doing all that yelling for I can't even get in there yet? (*Stopping and thinking.*) Cheque coming today?

Ruth   They *said* Saturday and this is just Friday and I hopes to God you ain't going to get up here first thing this morning and start talking to me 'bout no money – 'cause I 'bout don't want to hear it.

Walter   Something the matter with you this morning?

Ruth   No – I'm just sleepy as the devil. What kind of eggs you want?

Walter   Not scrambled. (**Ruth** *starts to scramble eggs.*) Paper come? (**Ruth** *points impatiently to the rolled up* Tribune *on the table, and he gets it and spreads it out and vaguely reads the front page.*) Set off another bomb yesterday.

Ruth (*maximum indifference*) Did they?

Walter (*looking up*)   What's the matter with you?

Ruth   Ain't nothing the matter with me. And don't keep asking me that this morning.

Walter   Ain't nobody bothering you. (*Reading the news of the day absently again.*) Say, Colonel McCormick is sick.

Ruth (*affecting tea-party interest*)   Is he now? Poor thing.

Walter (*sighing and looking at his watch*)   Oh, me. (*He waits.*) Now what is that boy doing in that bathroom all this time? He just going to have to start getting up earlier. I can't be being late to work on account of him fooling around in there.

Ruth (*turning on him*)   Oh, no, he ain't going to be getting up no earlier no such thing! It ain't his fault that he can't get to bed no earlier nights 'cause he got a bunch of crazy good-for-nothing clowns sitting up running their mouths in what is supposed to be his bedroom after ten o'clock at night . . .

Walter   That's what you mad about, ain't it? The things I want to talk about with my friends just couldn't be important in your mind, could they?

He rises and finds a cigarette in her handbag on the table and crosses to the little window and looks out, smoking and deeply enjoying this first one.

Ruth (*almost matter of factly, a complaint too automatic to deserve emphasis*)   Why you always got to smoke before you eat in the morning?

Walter (*at the window*)   Just look at 'em down there . . . Running and racing to work . . . (*He turns and faces his wife and watches her a moment at the stove, and then, suddenly.*) You look young this morning, baby.

Ruth (*indifferently*)   Yeah?

Walter   Just for a second – stirring them eggs. It's gone now – just for a second it was – you looked real young again. (*Then drily.*) Its gone now – you look like yourself again.

Ruth   Man, if you don't shut up and leave me alone.

Walter (*looking out to the street again*) First thing a man ought to learn in life is not to make love to no coloured woman first thing in the morning. You all some evil people at eight o'clock in the morning.

Travis *appears in the hall doorway, almost fully dressed and quite wide awake now, his towels and pyjamas across his shoulders. He opens the door and signals for his father to make the bathroom in a hurry.*

Travis (*watching the bathroom*)   Daddy, come on!

Walter *gets his bathroom utensils and flies out to the bathroom.*

Ruth   Sit down and have your breakfast, Travis.

Travis   Mama, this is Friday. (*Gleefully.*) Cheque coming tomorrow, huh?

Ruth   You get your mind off money and eat your breakfast.

Travis (*eating*)   This is the morning we supposed to bring the fifty cents to school.

Ruth   Well, I ain't got no fifty cents this morning.

Travis   Teacher say we have to.

Ruth   I don't care what teacher say. I ain't got it. Eat your breakfast, Travis.

Travis   I *am* eating.

Ruth   Hush up now and just eat!

The boy gives her an exasperated look for her lack of understanding, and eats grudgingly.

Travis   You think Grandmama would have it?

Ruth   No! And I want you to stop asking your grandmother for money, you hear me?

Travis (*outraged*)   Gaaaleee! I don't ask her, she just gimme it sometimes!

Ruth   Travis Willard Younger – I got too much on me this morning to be –

Travis   Maybe Daddy –

Ruth   *Travis!*

The boy hushes abruptly. They are both quiet and tense for several seconds.

Travis (*presently*)   Could I maybe go carry some groceries in front of the supermarket for a little while after school then?

Ruth   Just hush, I said. (**Travis** *jabs his spoon into his cereal bowl viciously, and rests his head in anger upon his fists.*) If you through eating, you can get over there and make up your bed.

The boy obeys stiffly and crosses the room, almost mechanically, to the bed and more or less carefully folds the covering. He carries the bedding into his mother's room and returns with his books and cap.

Travis (*sulking and standing apart from her unnaturally*)   I'm gone.

Ruth (*looking up from the stove to inspect him automatically*) Come here. (*He crosses to her and she studies his head.*) If you don't take this comb and fix this here head, you better! (**Travis** *puts down his books with a great sigh of oppression, and crosses to the mirror. His mother mutters under her breath about his 'stubborness'.*) 'Bout to march out of here with that head looking just like chickens slept in it! I just don't know where you get your slubborn ways . . . And get your jacket, too. Looks chilly out this morning.

Travis (*with conspicuously brushed hair and jacket*)   I'm gone.

Ruth   Get car-fare and milk money (*waving one finger*) and not a single penny for no caps, you hear me?

Travis (*with sullen politeness*)   Yes'm.

He turns in outrage to leave. His mother watches him as in his frustration he approaches the door almost comically. When she speaks to him, her voice has become a very gentle tease.

Ruth (*mocking; as she thinks he would say it*)   Oh, Mama makes me so mad sometimes, I don't know what to do! (*She waits and continues to his back as he stands stock-still in front of the door.*) I wouldn't kiss that woman good-bye for nothing in this world this morning! (*The boy finally turns round and rolls his eyes at her, knowing the mood has changed and he is vindicated; he does not,*

however, move towards her yet.) Not for nothing in this world!
(*She finally laughs aloud at him and holds out her arms and we see that
it is a way between them, very old and practised. He crosses to her and
allows her to embrace him warmly but keeps his face fixed with
masculine rigidity. She holds him back from her presently and looks at
him and runs her fingers over the features of his face. With utter
gentleness.*) Now – whose little old angry man are you?

Travis (*the masculinity and gruffness start to fade at last*)   Aw
gaalee – Mama . . .

Ruth (*mimicking*)   Aw – gaaaaalleeeee, Mama! (*She pushes
him, with rough playfulness and finality, towards the door.*) Get on
out of here or you going to be late.

Travis (*in the face of love, new aggressiveness*) Mama, could I
please go carry groceries?

Ruth   Honey, it's starting to get so cold evenings.

Walter (*coming in from the bathroom and drawing a make-believe
gun from a make-believe holster and shooting at his son*)   What is it
he wants to do?

Ruth   Go carry groceries after school at the supermarket.

Walter   Well, let him go . . .

Travis (*quickly, to the ally*)   I *have* to – she won't gimme the
fifty cents . . .

Walter (*to his wife only*)   Why not?

Ruth (*simply, and with flavour*)   'Cause we don't have it.

Walter (*to* **Ruth** *only*)   What you tell the boys things like
that for? (*Reaching down into his pants with a rather important
gesture.*) Here, son –

He hands the boy the coin, but his eyes are directed to his wife's.
Travis *takes the money happily.*

Travis   Thanks, Daddy.

He starts out. **Ruth** *watches both of them with murder in her eyes.*
Walter *stands and stares back at her with defiance, and suddenly
reaches into his pocket as an afterthought.*

Walter (*without even looking at his son, still staring hard at his wife*)
In fact, there's another fifty cents . . . Buy yourself some fruit
today – or take a taxi-cab to school or something!

Travis   Whoopee –

*He leaps up and clasps his father around the middle with his legs, and
they face each other in mutual appreciation; slowly* **Walter Lee**
*peeps around the boy to catch the violent rays from his wife's eyes and
draws his head back as if shot.*

Walter   You better get down now – and get to school,
man.

Travis (*at the door*)   O.K. Good-bye.

He goes.

Walter (*after him, pointing with pride*)   That's *my* boy. (*She
looks at him in disgust and turns back to her work.*) You know what
I was thinking 'bout in the bathroom this morning?

Ruth   No.

Walter   How come you always try to be so pleasant?

Ruth   What is there to be pleasant 'bout?

Walter   You want to know what I was thinking 'bout in
the bathroom or not?

Ruth   I know what you was thinking 'bout.

Walter (*ignoring her*)   'Bout what me and Willy Harris was
talking about last night.

Ruth (*immediately – a refrain*)   Willy Harris is a good-for-
nothing loud mouth.

Walter   Anybody who talks to me has got to be a good-
for-nothing loud mouth, ain't he? And what you know
about who is just a good-for-nothing loud mouth? Charlie

Atkins was just a 'good-for-nothing loud mouth' too, wasn't he? When he wanted me to go in the dry-cleaning business with him. And now – he's grossing a hundred thousand a year. A hundred thousand dollars a year! You still call *him* a loud mouth!

Ruth (*bitterly*)   Oh, Walter Lee . . .

She folds her head on her arms over on the table.

Walter (*rising and coming to her and standing over her.*)   You tired, ain't you? Tired of everything. Me, the boy, the way we live – this beat-up hole – everything. Ain't you? (*She doesn't look up, doesn't answer.*) So tired – moaning and groaning all the time, but you wouldn't do nothing to help, would you? You couldn't be on my side that long for nothing, could you?

Ruth   Walter, please leave me alone.

Walter   A man needs for a woman to back him up . . .

Ruth   Walter –

Walter   Mama would listen to you. You know she listen to you more than she do me and Bennie. She think more of you. All you have to do is just sit down with her when you drinking your coffee one morning and talking 'bout things like you do and (*he sits down beside her and demonstrates graphically what he thinks her methods and tone should be*) you just sip your coffee, see, and say easy like that you been thinking 'bout that deal Walter Lee is so interested in, 'bout the store and all, and sip some more coffee, like what you saying ain't really that important to you . . . And the next thing you know, she be listening good and asking you questions and when I come home – I can tell her the details. This ain't no fly-by-night proposition, baby. I mean we figure it out, me and Willy and Bobo.

Ruth (*with a frown*)   Bobo?

Walter   Yeah. You see, this little liquor store we got in mind cost seventy-five thousand and we figured the initial investment on the place be 'bout thirty thousand, see. That be ten thousand each. Course, there's a couple of hundred you got to pay so's you don't spend your life just waiting for them clowns to let your licence get approved –

Ruth   You mean graft?

Walter (*frowning impatiently*) Don't call it that. See there, that just goes to show you what women understand about the world. Baby, don't *nothing* happen for you in this world 'less you pay *somebody* off!

Ruth   Walter, leave me alone! (*She raises her head and stares at him vigorously – then says, more quietly.*) Eat your eggs, they gonna be cold.

Walter (*straightening up from her and looking off*)   That's it. There you are. Man say to his woman: I got me a dream. His woman say: Eat your eggs. (*Sadly, but gaining in power.*) Man say: I got to take hold of this here world, baby! And a woman will say: Eat your eggs and go to work. (*Passionately now.*) Man say: I got to change my life, I'm choking to death, baby! And his woman say (*in utter anguish as he brings his fists down on his thighs*) Your eggs is getting cold!

Ruth (*softly*)   Walter, that ain't none of our money.

Walter (*not listening at all or even looking at her*)   This morning, I was lookin' in the mirror and thinking about it . . . I'm thirty-five years old; I been married eleven years and I got a boy who sleeps in the living-room (*very, very quietly*) and all I got to give him is stories about how rich white people live . . .

Ruth   Eat your eggs, Walter.

Walter   *Damn my eggs . . . damn all the eggs that ever was!*

Ruth   Then go to work.

Walter (*looking up at her*)   See – I'm trying to talk to you 'bout myself (*shaking his head with the repetition*) and all you can say is eat them eggs and go to work.

Ruth (*wearily*)   Honey, you never say nothing new. I listen to you every day, every night and every morning, and you never say nothing new. (*Shrugging.*) So you would rather *be* Mr. Arnold than be his chauffeur. So – I would *rather* be living in Buckingham Palace.

Walter   That is just what is wrong with the coloured women in this world . . . Don't understand about building their men up and making 'em feel like they somebody. Like they can do something.

Ruth (*drily, but to hurt*)   There *are* coloured men who do things.

Walter   No thanks to the coloured woman.

Ruth   Well, being a coloured woman, I guess I can't help myself none.

She rises and gets the ironing board and sets it up and attacks a huge pile of rough-dried clothes, sprinkling them in preparation for the ironing and then rolling them into tight fat balls.

Walter (*mumbling*)   We one group of men tied to a race of women with small minds.

*His sister **Beneatha** enters. She is about twenty, as slim and intense as her brother. She is not as pretty as her sister-in-law, but her lean, almost intellectual face has a handsomeness of its own. She wears a bright-red flannel nightie, and her thick hair stands wildly about her head. Her speech is a mixture of many things; it is different from the rest of the family's insofar as education has permeated her sense of English – and perhaps the Mid-west rather than the South has finally – at last – won out in her inflexion; but not altogether, because over all of it is a soft slurring and transformed use of vowels which is the decided influence of the Southside. She passes through the room without looking at either **Ruth** or **Walter** and goes to the outside door and looks, a little blindly, out to the bathroom. She sees that it has been lost to the Johnsons. She closes the door with a sleepy vengeance and crosses to the table and sits down a little defeated.*

Beneatha   I am going to start timing those people.

Walter   You should get up earlier.

Beneatha (*her face in her hands. She is still fighting the urge to go back to bed*)   Really – would you suggest dawn? Where's the paper?

Walter (*pushing the paper across the table to her as he studies her almost clinically, as though he has never seen her before*)   You a horrible-looking chick at this hour.

Beneatha (*drily*)   Good morning, everybody.

Walter (*senselessly*)   How is school coming?

Beneatha (*in the same spirit*)   Lovely. Lovely. And you know, biology is the greatest. (*Looking up at him.*) I dissected something that looked just like you yesterday.

Walter   I just wondered if you've made up your mind and everything.

Beneatha (*gaining in sharpness and impatience*)   And what did I answer yesterday morning – and the day before that?

Ruth (*from the ironing board, like someone disinterested and old*) Don't be so nasty, Bennie.

Beneatha (*still to her brother*)   And the day before that the day before that!

Walter (*defensively*)   I'm interested in you. Something wrong with that? Ain't many girls who decide . . .

Walter *and* **Beneatha** (*in unison*)   . . . 'to be a doctor.'

Silence.

Walter   Have we figured out yet just exactly how much medical school is going to cost?

Ruth   Walter Lee, why don't you leave that girl alone and get out of here to work?

Beneatha (*goes out to the bathroom and bangs on the door*) Come on out of there, please!

She comes back into the room.

Walter (*looking at his sister intently*)   You know the cheque is coming tomorrow.

Beneatha (*turning on him with a sharpness all her own*)   That money belongs to Mama, Walter, and it's for her to decide how she wants to use it. I don't care if she wants to buy a house or a rocket ship or just nail it up somewhere and look at it. It's hers. Not ours – *hers*.

Walter (*bitterly*)   Now ain't that fine! You just got your mother's interest at heart, ain't you, girl? You such a nice girl – but if Mama got that money she can always take a few thousand and help you through school too – can't she?

Beneatha   I have never asked anyone around here to do anything for me!

Walter   No! And the line between asking and just accepting when the time comes is big and wide – ain't it!

Beneatha (*with fury*)   What do you want from me, Brother – that I quit school or just drop dead, which?

Walter   I don't want nothing but for you to stop acting holy 'round here. Me and Ruth done made some sacrifices for you – why can't you do something for the family?

Ruth   Walter, don't be dragging me in it.

Walter   You are in it. Don't you get up and go work in somebody's kitchen for the last three years to help put clothes on her back?

Ruth   Oh, Walter – that's not fair . . .

Walter   It ain't that nobody expects you to get on your knees and say thank you, Brother; thank you, Ruth; thank you, Mama – and thank you, Travis, for wearing the same pair of shoes for two semesters –

Beneatha (*dropping to her knees*)   Well – I *do* – all right? – thank everybody . . . and forgive me for ever wanting to be anything at all . . . forgive me, forgive me!

Ruth   Please stop it! Your Mama'll hear you.

Walter   Who the hell told you you had to be a doctor? If you so crazy 'bout messing 'round with sick people – then go be a nurse like other women – or just get married and be quiet . . .

Beneatha   Well – you finally got it said . . . It took you three years but you finally got it said. Walter, give up; leave me alone – it's Mama's money.

Walter   *He was my father, too!*

Beneatha   So what? He was mine, too – and Travis's grandfather – but the insurance money belongs to Mama. Picking on me is not going to make her give it to you to invest in any liquor stores (*under her breath, dropping into a chair*) and I for one say, God bless Mama for that!

Walter (*to* **Ruth**)   See – did you hear? Did you hear?

Ruth   Honey, please go to work.

Walter   Nobody in this house is ever going to understand me.

Beneatha   Because you're a nut.

Walter   Who's a nut?

Beneatha   You – you are a nut. Thee is mad, boy.

Walter (*looking at his wife and his sister from the door, very sadly*) The world's most backward race of people, and that's a fact.

Beneatha (*turning slowly in her chair*)   And then there are all those prophets who would lead us out of the wilderness (**Walter** *slams out of the house*) into the swamps!

Ruth   Bennie, why you always gotta be pickin' on your brother? Can't you be a little sweeter sometimes? (*Door opens.* **Walter** *walks in.*)

Walter (*to* **Ruth**)   I need some money for car-fare.

Ruth (*looks at him, then warms; teasing, but tenderly*)   Fifty cents? (*She goes to her bag and gets money.*) Here, take a taxi.

Walter *goes.* **Mama** *enters. She is a woman in her early sixties, full-bodied and strong. She is one of those women of a certain grace and beauty who wear it so unobtrusively that it takes a while to notice. Her dark-brown face is surrounded by the total whiteness of her hair, and, being a woman who has adjusted to many things in life and overcome many more, her face is full of strength. She has, we can see, wit and faith of a kind that keep her eyes lit and full of interest and expectancy. She is, in a world, a beautiful woman. Her bearing is perhaps most like the noble bearing of the women of the Hereros of South-west Africa – rather as if she imagines that as she walks she still bears a basket or a vessel upon her head. Her speech, on the other hand, is as careless as her carriage is precise – she is inclined to slur everything – but her voice is perhaps not so much quiet as simply soft.*

Mama   Who that 'round here slamming doors at this hour?

She crosses through the room, goes to the window, opens it, and brings a feeble little plant growing doggedly in a small pot on the window sill. She feels the dirt and puts it back out.

Ruth   That was Walter Lee. He and Bennie was at it again.

Mama   My children and they tempers. Lord, if this little old plant don't get more sun than it's been getting it ain't never going to see spring again. (*She turns from the window.*) What's the matter with you this morning, Ruth? You looks right peaked. You aiming to iron all them things? Leave some for me. I'll get to 'em this afternoon. Bennie honey, it's too draughty for you to be sitting 'round half dressed. Where's your robe?

Beneatha   In the cleaners.

Mama   Well, go get mine and put it on.

Beneatha   I'm not cold, Mama, honest.

Mama   I know – but you so thin . . .

Beneatha (*irritably*)   Mama, I'm not cold.

Mama (*seeing the make-down bed as* **Travis** *has left it*)   Lord have mercy, look at that poor bed. Bless his heart – he tries, don't he?

Ruth   No – he don't half try at all 'cause he knows you going to come along behind him and fix everything. That's just how come he don't know how to do nothing right now – you done spoiled that boy so.

Mama   Well – he's a little boy. Ain't supposed to know 'bout housekeeping. My baby, that's what he is. What you fix for his breakfast this morning?

Ruth (*angrily*)   I feed my son, Lena!

Mama   I ain't meddling. (*Under her breath; busy-bodyish.*) I just noticed all last week he had cold cereal, and when it starts getting this chilly in the fall a child ought to have some hot grits or something when he goes out in the cold –

Ruth (*furious*)   I gave him hot oats – is that all right?

Mama   I ain't meddling. (*Pause*) Put a lot of nice butter on it? (**Ruth** *shoots her an angry look and does not reply.*) He likes lots of butter.

Ruth (*exasperated*)   Lena –

Mama (*to* **Beneatha**. **Mama** *is inclined to wander conversationally sometimes*)   What was you and your brother fussing 'bout this morning?

Beneatha   It's not important, Mama.

She gets up and goes to look out at the bathroom, which is apparently free, and she picks up her towels and rushes out.

Mama   What was they fighting about?

Ruth   Now you know as well as I do.

Mama (*shaking her head*)   Brother still worrying hisself sick about that money?

Ruth   You know he is.

Mama   You had breakfast?

Ruth   Some coffee.

Mama   Girl, you better start eating and looking after yourself better. You almost thin as Travis.

Ruth   Lena –

Mama   Uh-hunh?

Ruth   What are you going to do with it?

Mama   Now don't you start, child. It's too early in the morning to be talking about money. It ain't Christian.

Ruth   It's just that he got his heart set on that store –

Mama   You mean that liquor store that Willy Harris want him to invest in?

Ruth   Yes –

Mama   We ain't no business people, Ruth. We just plain working folks.

Ruth   Ain't nobody business people till they go into business. Walter Lee say coloured people ain't never going to start getting ahead till they start gambling on some different kinds of things in the world – investments and things.

Mama   What done got into you, girl? Walter Lee done finally sold you on investing.

Ruth   No, Mama, something is happening between Walter and me. I don't know what it is – but he needs something – something I can't give him any more. He needs this chance, Lena.

Mama (*frowning deeply*)   But liquor, honey –

Ruth   Well – like Walter say – I spec people going to always be drinking themselves some liquor.

Mama   Well – whether they drinks it or not ain't none of my business. But whether I go into business selling it to 'em *is*, and I don't want that on my ledger this late in life. (*Stopping suddenly and studying her daughter-in-law.*) Ruth Younger, what's the matter with you today? You look like you could fall over right there.

Ruth   I'm tired.

Mama   Then you better stay home from work today.

Ruth   I can't stay home. She'd be calling up the agency and screaming at them, 'My girl didn't come in today – send me somebody! My girl didn't come in!' Oh, she just have a fit . . .

Mama   Well, let her have it. I'll just call her up and say you got the flu –

Ruth (*laughing*)   Why the flu?

Mama   'Cause it sounds respectable to 'em. Something white people get, too. They know 'bout the flu. Otherwise they think you been cut up or something when you tell 'em you sick.

Ruth   I got to go in. We need the money.

Mama   Somebody would of thought my children done all but starved to death the way they talk about money here late. Child, we got a great big old cheque coming tomorrow.

Ruth (*sincerely, but also self-righteously*)   Now that's your money. It ain't got nothing to do with me. We all feel like that – Walter and Bennie and me – even Travis.

Mama (*thoughtfully, and suddenly very far away*)   Ten thousand dollars –

Ruth   Sure is wonderful.

Mama   Ten thousand dollars.

Ruth   You know what you should do, Miss Lena? You should take yourself a trip somewhere. To Europe or South America or someplace –

Mama (*throwing up her hands at the thought*)   Oh, child!

Ruth   I'm serious. Just pack up and leave! Go on away and enjoy yourself some. Forget about the family and have yourself a ball for once in your life –

Mama (*drily*)   You sound like I'm just about ready to die. Who'd go with me? What I look like wandering 'round Europe by myself?

Ruth   Shoot – these here rich white women do it all the time. They don't think nothing of packing up they suitcases and piling on one of them big steamships and – swoosh! – they gone, child.

Mama   Something always told me I wasn't no rich white woman.

Ruth   Well – what are you going to do with it then?

Mama   I ain't rightly decided. (*Thinking. She speaks now with emphasis.*) Some of it got to be put away for Beneatha and her schoolin' – and ain't nothing going to touch that part of it. Nothing. (*She waits several seconds, trying to make up her mind about something, and looks at* **Ruth** *a little tentatively before going on.*) Been thinking that we maybe could meet the notes on a little old two-storey somewhere, with a yard where Travis could play in the summer-time, if we use part of the insurance for a down payment and everybody kind of pitch in. I could maybe take on a little day work again, few days a week –

Ruth (*studying her mother-in-law furtively and concentrating on her ironing, anxious to encourage without seeming to*)   Well, Lord knows, we've put enough rent into this here rat trap to pay for four houses by now . . .

Mama (*looking up at the words 'rat trap' and then looking around and leaning back and sighing – in a suddenly reflective mood*)   'Rat trap' – yes, that's all it is. (*Smiling.*) I remember just as well the day me and Big Walter moved in here. Hadn't been married but two weeks and wasn't planning on living here no more than a year. (*She shakes her head at the dissolved dream.*) We was going to set away, little by little, don't you know, and buy a little place out in Morgan Park. We had even picked out the house. (*Chuckling a little.*) Looks right dumpy today. But Lord, child, you should know all the dreams I had 'bout buying that house and fixing it up and making me a little garden in the back – (*She waits and stops smiling.*) And didn't none of it happen. (*She drops her hands in a futile gesture.*)

Ruth (*keeps her head down, ironing*)   Yes, life can be a barrel of disappointments, sometimes.

Mama   Honey, Big Walter would come in here some nights back then and slump down on that couch there and just look at the rug, and look at me and look at the rug and then back at me – and I'd know he was down then . . . really down. (*After a second very long and thoughtful pause; she is seeing back to times that only she can see.*) And then, Lord, when I lost that baby – little Claude – I almost thought I was going to lose Big Walter too. Oh, that man grieved hisself! He was one man to love his children.

Ruth   Ain't nothin' can tear at you like losin' your baby.

Mama   I guess that's how come that man finally worked hisself to death like he done. Like he was fighting his own war with this here world that took his baby from him.

Ruth   He sure was a fine man, all right. I always liked Mr. Younger.

Mama   Crazy 'bout his children! God knows there was plenty wrong with Walter Younger – hard-headed, mean, kind of wild with women – plenty wrong with him. But he sure loved his children. Always wanted them to have something – be something. That's where Brother gets all these notions, I reckon. Big Walter used to say, he'd get right wet in the eyes sometimes, lean his head back with the water standing in his eyes and say, 'Seem like God didn't see fit to give the black man nothing but dreams – but He did give us children to make them dreams seem worth while.' (*She smiles.*) He could talk like that, don't you know.

Ruth   Yes, he sure could. He was a good man, Mr. Younger.

Mama   Yes, a fine man – just couldn't never catch up with his dreams, that's all.

Beneatha *comes in, brushing her hair and looking up to the ceiling, where the sound of a vacuum cleaner has started up.*

Beneatha   What could be so dirty on that woman's rugs that she has to vacuum them every single day?

Ruth   I wish certain young women 'round here who I could name would take inspiration about certain rugs in a certain apartment I could also mention.

Beneatha (*shrugging*)   How much cleaning can a house need, for Christ's sakes.

Mama (*not liking the Lord's name used thus*)   Bennie!

Ruth   Just listen to her – just listen!

Beneatha   Oh, God!

Mama   If you use the Lord's name just one more time –

Beneatha (*a bit of a whine*)   Oh, Mama –

Ruth   Fresh – just fresh as salt, this girl!

Beneatha (*drily*)   Well – if the salt loses its savour –

Mama   Now that will do. I just ain't going to have you 'round here reciting the scriptures in vain – you hear me?

Beneatha   How did I manage to get on everybody's wrong side by just walking into a room?

Ruth   If you weren't so fresh –

Beneatha   Ruth, I'm twenty years old.

Mama   What time you be home from school today?

Beneatha   Kind of late. (*With enthusiasm.*) Madeline is going to start my guitar lessons today.

Mama *and* **Ruth** *look up with the same expression.*

Mama   Your *what* kind of lessons?

Beneatha   Guitar.

Ruth   Oh, Father!

Mama   How come you done taken it in your mind to learn to play the guitar?

Beneatha   I just want to, that's all.

Mama (*smiling*)   Lord, child, don't you know what to do with yourself? How long it going to be before you get tired of this now – like you got tired of that little play-acting group you joined last year? (*Looking at* **Ruth**) And what was it the year before that?

Ruth   The horseback-riding club for which she bought that fifty-five dollar riding habit that's been hanging in the closet ever since!

Mama (*to* **Beneatha**)   Why you got to flit so from one thing to another, baby?

Beneatha (*sharply*)   I just want to learn to play the guitar. Is there anything wrong with that?

Mama   Ain't nobody trying to stop you. I just wonders sometimes why you has to flit so from one thing to another all the time. You ain't never done nothing with all that camera equipment you brought home –

Beneatha   I don't flit! I – I experiment with different forms of expression –

Ruth   Like riding a horse?

Beneatha   People have to express themselves one way or another.

Mama   What is it you want to express?

Beneatha (*angrily*)   Me! (**Mama** *and* **Ruth** *look at each other and burst into raucous laughter.*) Don't worry – I don't expect you to understand.

Mama (*to change the subject*)   Who you going out with tomorrow night?

Beneatha (*with displeasure*)   George Murchison again.

Mama (*pleased*)   Oh – you getting a little sweet on him?

Ruth   You ask me, this child ain't sweet on nobody but herself. (*Under her breath.*) Express herself!

They laugh.

Beneatha   Oh – I like George all right, Mama. I mean I like him enough to go out with him and stuff, but –

Ruth (*for devilment*)   What does *and stuff* mean?

Beneatha   Mind your own business.

Mama   Stop picking at her now, Ruth. (*A thoughtful pause, and then a suspicious sudden look at her daughter as she turns in her chair for emphasis.*) What *does* it mean?

Beneatha (*wearily*)   Oh, I just mean I couldn't ever really be serious about George. He's – he's so shallow.

Ruth   Shallow – what do you mean he's shallow? He's *rich!*

Mama   Hush, Ruth.

Beneatha   I know he's rich. He knows he's rich, too.

Ruth   Well – what other qualities a man got to have to satisfy you, little girl?

Beneatha   You wouldn't even begin to understand. Anybody who married Walter could not possibly understand.

Mama (*outraged*)   What kind of way is that to talk about your brother?

Beneatha   Brother is a flip – let's face it.

Mama (*to* **Ruth**, *helplessly*)   What's a flip?

Ruth (*glad to add kindling*)   She's saying he's crazy.

Beneatha   Not crazy. Brother isn't really crazy yet – he – he's an elaborate neurotic.

Mama   Hush your mouth!

Beneatha   As for George. Well. George looks good – he's got a beautiful car and he takes me to nice places and, as my sister-in-law says, he is probably the richest boy I will ever get to know and I even like him sometimes – but if the Youngers are sitting around waiting to see if their little Bennie is going to tie up the family with the Murchisons, they are wasting their time.

Ruth   You mean you wouldn't marry George Murchison if he asked you someday? That pretty, rich thing? Honey, I knew you was odd –

Beneatha   No I would not marry him if all I felt for him was what I feel now. Besides, George's family wouldn't really like it.

Mama   Why not?

Beneatha   Oh, Mama – the Murchisons are honest-to-God-real-*live*-rich coloured people, and the only people in the world who are more snobbish than rich white people are rich coloured people. I thought everybody knew that. I've met Mrs. Murchison. She's a scene!

Mama   You must not dislike people 'cause they well off, honey.

Beneatha   Why not? It makes just as much sense as disliking people 'cause they are poor, and lots of people do that.

Ruth (*a wisdom-of-the-ages manner. To* **Mama**)   Well, she'll get over some of this –

Beneatha   Get over it? What are you talking about, Ruth? Listen, I'm going to be a doctor. I'm not worried about who I'm going to marry yet – if I ever get married.

Mama *and* **Ruth**   *If!*

Mama   Now, Bennie –

Beneatha   Oh, I probably will . . . but first I'm going to be a doctor, and George, for one, still thinks that's pretty funny. I couldn't be bothered with that. I am going to be a doctor and everybody around here better understand that!

Mama (*kindly*)   'Course you going to be a doctor, honey, God willing.

Beneatha (*drily*)   God hasn't got a thing to do with it.

Mama   Beneatha – that just wasn't necessary.

Beneatha   Well – neither is God. I get sick of hearing about God.

Mama   Beneatha!

Beneatha   I mean it! I'm just tired of hearing about God all the time. What has He got to do with anything? Does he pay tuition?

Mama   You 'bout to get your fresh little jaw slapped!

Ruth   That's just what she needs, all right!

Beneatha   Why? Why can't I say what I want to around here, like everybody else?

Mama   It don't sound nice for a young girl to say things like that – you wasn't brought up that way. Me and your father went to trouble to get you and Brother to church every Sunday.

Beneatha   Mama, you don't understand. It's all a matter of ideas, and God is just one idea I don't accept. It's not important. I am not going out and be immoral or commit crimes because I don't believe in God. I don't even think about it. It's just that I get tired of Him getting credit for all the things the human race achieves through its own stubborn effort. There simply is no blasted God – there is only man and it is he who makes miracles!

Mama *absorbs this speech, studies her daughter and rises slowly and crosses to* **Beneatha** *and slaps her powerfully across the face. After, there is only silence and the daughter drops her eyes from her mother's face, and* **Mama** *is very tall before her.*

Mama   Now – you say after me, in my mother's house there is still God. (*There is a long pause and* **Beneatha** *stares at the floor wordlessly.* **Mama** *repeats the phrase with precision and cool emotion.*) In my mother's house there is still God.

Beneatha   In my mother's house there is still God.

A long pause.

Mama (*walking away from* **Beneatha**, *too disturbed for triumphant posture. Stopping and turning back to her daughter*) There are some ideas we ain't going to have in this house. Not long as I am at the head of this family.

Beneatha   Yes, ma'am.

Mama *walks out of the room.*

Ruth (*almost gently, with profound understanding*)   You think you a woman, Bennie – but you still a little girl. What you did was childish – so you got treated like a child.

Beneatha   I see. (*Quietly.*) I also see that everybody thinks it's all right for Mama to be a tyrant. But all the tyranny in the world will never put a God in the heavens!

She picks up her books and goes out.

Ruth (*goes to* **Mama***'s door*)   She said she was sorry.

Mama (*coming out, going to her plant*)   They frightens me, Ruth. My children.

Ruth   You got good children, Lena. They just a little off sometimes – but they're good.

Mama   No – there's something come down between me and them that don't let us understand each other and I don't know what it is. One done almost lost his mind thinking 'bout money all the time and the other done commence to talk about things I can't seem to understand in no form or fashion. What is it that's changing, Ruth?

Ruth (*soothingly, older than her years*)   Now . . . you taking it all too seriously. You just got strong-willed children and it takes a strong woman like you to keep 'em in hand.

Mama (*looking at her plant and sprinkling a little water on it*)   They spirited all right, my children. Got to admit they got spirit – Bennie and Walter. Like this little old plant that ain't never had enough sunshine or nothing – and look at it . . .

She has her back to **Ruth**, *who has to stop ironing and lean against something and put the back of hand to her forehead.*

Ruth (*trying to keep* **Mama** *from noticing*)   You . . . sure . . . loves that little old thing, don't you? . . .

Mama   Well, I always wanted me a garden like I used to see sometimes at the back of the houses down home. This plant is close as I ever got to having one. (*She looks out of the window as she replaces the plant.*) Lord, ain't nothing as dreary as the view from this window on a dreary day, is there? Why ain't you singing this morning, Ruth? Sing that 'No Ways Tired'. That song always lifts me up so. (*She turns at last to see* *that* **Ruth** *has slipped quietly into a chair, in a state of semiconsciousness.*) Ruth! Ruth honey – what's the matter with you . . . Ruth!

Curtain.

Scene Two

It is the following morning; a Saturday morning, and house cleaning is in progress at the **Youngers***. Furniture has been shoved hither and yon and* **Mama** *is giving the kitchen-area walls a washing down.* **Beneatha***, in dungarees, with a handkerchief tied around her face, is spraying insecticide into the cracks in the walls. As they work, the radio is on and a Southside disc-jokey programme is inappropriately filling the house with a rather exotic saxophone blues.* **Travis***, is the sole idle one, is leaning on his arms, looking out of the window.*

Travis   Grandmama, that stuff Bennie is using smells awful. Can I go downstairs, please?

Mama   Did you get all them chores done already? I ain't seen you doing much.

Travis   Yes'm – finished early. Where did Mama go this morning.

Mama (*looking at* **Beneatha**)   She had to go on a little errand.

Travis   Where?

Mama   To tend to her business.

Travis   Can I go outside then?

Mama   Oh, I guess so. You better stay right in front of the house, though . . . and keep a good lookout for the postman.

Travis   Yes'm. (*He starts out and decides to give his* **Aunt Beneatha** *a good swat on the legs as he passes her.*)   Leave them poor little old cockroaches alone, they ain't bothering you none.

He runs as she swings the spray gun at him both viciously and playfully. **Walter** *enters from the bedroom and goes to the phone.*

Mama   Look out there, girl, before you be spilling some of that stuff on that child!

Travis (*teasing*)   That's right – look out now!

He goes.

Beneatha (*drily*)   I can't imagine that it would hurt him – it has never hurt the roaches.

Mama   Well, little boys' hides ain't as tough as Southside roaches.

Walter (*into phone*)   Hello – Let me talk to Willy Harris.

Mama   You better get over there behind the bureau. I seen one marching out of there like Napoleon yesterday.

Walter   Hello, Willy? It ain't come yet. It'll be here in a few minutes. Did the lawyer give you the papers?

Beneatha   There's really only one way to get rid of them Mama –

Mama   How?

Beneatha   Set fire to this building.

Walter   Good. Good. I'll be right over.

Beneatha   Where did Ruth go, Walter?

Walter   I don't know.

He goes out abruptly.

Beneatha   Mama, where did Ruth go?

Mama (*looking at her with meaning*)   To the doctor, I think.

Beneatha   The doctor? What's the matter? (*They exchange glances.*) You don't think –

Mama (*with her sense of drama*)   Now I ain't saying what I think. But I ain't never been wrong 'bout a woman neither.

The phone rings.

Beneatha (*at the phone*)   Hay-lo . . . (*Pause, and a moment of recognition.*) Well – when did you get back? . . . And how was it? . . . Of course I've missed you – in my way . . . This morning? No . . . house cleaning and all that and Mama hates it if I let people come over when the house is like this . . . You *have?* Well, that's different . . . What is it – Oh, what the hell, come on over . . . Right, see you then. (*She hangs up.*)

Mama (*who has listened vigorously, as is her habit*)   Who is that you inviting over here with this house looking like this? You ain't got the pride you was born with!

Beneatha   Asagai doesn't care how houses look, Mama – he's an intellectual.

Mama   *Who?*

Beneatha   Asagai – Joseph Asagai. He's an African boy I met on campus. He's been studying in Canada all summer.

Mama   What's his name?

Beneatha   Asagai, Joseph. Ah-sah-guy . . . He's from Nigeria.

Mama   Oh, that's the little country that was founded by slaves way back . . .

Beneatha   No, Mama – that's Liberia.

Mama   I don't think I never met no African before.

Beneatha   Well, do me a favour and don't ask him a whole lot of ignorant questions about Africans. I mean, do they wear clothes and all that –

Mama   Well, now, I guess if you think we so ignorant 'round here maybe you shouldn't bring your friends here –

Beneatha   It's just that people ask such crazy things. All anyone seems to know about when it comes to Africa is Tarzan –

Mama (*indignantly*)   Why should I know anything about Africa?

Beneatha   Why do you give money at church for the missionary work?

Mama   Well, that's to help save people.

Beneatha   You mean save them from *heathenism* –

Mama (*innocently*)   Yes.

Beneatha   I'm afraid they need more salvation from the British and the French.

Ruth *comes in forlornly and pulls off her coat with dejection. They both look at her.*

Ruth (*dispiritedly*)   Well, I guess from all the happy faces – everybody knows.

Beneatha   You pregnant?

Mama   Lord have mercy, I sure hope it's a little old girl. Travis ought to have a sister.

Beneatha *and* **Ruth** *give her a hopeless look for this grandmotherly enthusiasm.*

Beneatha   How far along are you?

Ruth   Two months.

Beneatha   Did you mean to? I mean did you plan it or was it an accident?

Mama   What do you know about planning or not planning?

Beneatha   Oh, Mama.

Ruth (*wearily*)   She's twenty years old, Lena.

Beneatha   Did you plan it, Ruth?

Ruth   Mind your own business.

Beneatha It is my business – where is he going to live, on the *roof*? (*There is silence following the remark as the three women react to the sense of it.*) Gee – I didn't mean that, Ruth, honest. Gee, I don't feel like that at all. I – I think it is wonderful.

Ruth (*dully*) Wonderful.

Beneatha Yes – really.

Mama (*looking at* **Ruth**, *worried*) Doctor say everything going to be all right?

Ruth (*far away*) Yes – she says everything is going to be fine . . .

Mama (*immediately suspicious*) 'She' – What doctor you went to?

Ruth *folds over, near hysteria.*

Mama (*worriedly hovering over* **Ruth**) Ruth honey – what's the matter with you – you sick?

Ruth *has her fists clenched on her thighs and is fighting hard to suppress a scream that seems to be rising in her.*

Beneatha What's the matter with her, Mama?

Mama (*working her fingers in* **Ruth**'s *shoulder to relax her*) She be all right. Women gets right depressed sometimes when they get her way. (*Speaking softly, expertly, rapidly.*) Now you just relax. That's right . . . just lean back, don't think 'bout nothing at all . . . nothing at all –

Ruth I'm all right . . .

The glassy-eyed look melts and then she collapses into a fit of heavy sobbing. The bell rings.

Beneatha Oh, my God – that must be Asagai.

Mama (*to* **Ruth**) Come on now, honey. You need to lie down and rest awhile . . . then have some nice hot food.

They go out, **Ruth***'s weight on her mother-in-law.* **Beneatha***, herself profoundly disturbed, opens the door to admit a rather dramatic-looking young man with a large package.*

Asagai   Hello, Alaiyo –

Beneatha (*holding the door open and regarding him with pleasure*) Hello . . . (*Long pause.*) Well – come in. And please excuse everything. My mother was very upset about my letting anyone come here with the place like this.

Asagai (*coming into the room*)   You look disturbed too . . . Is something wrong?

Beneatha (*still at the door, absently*)   Yes . . . we've all got acute ghetto-itus. (*She smiles and comes towards him, finding a cigarette and sitting.*) So – sit down! How was Canada?

Asagai (*a sophisticate*)   Canadian.

Beneatha (*looking at him*)   I'm very glad you are back.

Asagai (*looking back at her in turn*)   Are you really?

Beneatha   Yes – very.

Asagai   Why – you were quite glad when I went away. What happened?

Beneatha   You went away.

Asagai   Ahhhhhhhhh.

Beneatha   Before – you wanted to be so serious before there was time.

Asagai   How much time must there be before one knows what one feels?

Beneatha (*stalling this particular conversation. Her hands pressed together, in a deliberate childish gesture.*)   What did you bring me?

Asagai (*handing her the package*)   Open it and see.

Beneatha (*eagerly opening the package and drawing out some records and the colourful robes of a Nigerian woman*)   Oh, Asagai! . . . You got them for me! . . . How beautiful . . . and the records too! (*She lifts out the robes and runs to the mirror with them and holds the drapery up in front of herself.*)

Asagai (*coming to her at the mirror*)   I shall have to teach you how to drape it properly. (*He flings the material about her for the moment and stands back to look at her.*) Ah – *Oh-pay-gay-day, oh-gbah-mu-shay* (*a Yoruba exclamation for admiration*). You wear it well . . . very well . . . mutilated hair and all.

Beneatha (*turning suddenly*)   My hair – what's wrong with my hair?

Asagai (*shrugging*) Were you born with it like that?

Beneatha (*reaching up to touch it*)   No . . . of course not. (*She looks back to the mirror, disturbed.*)

Asagai (*smiling*)   How then?

Beneatha   You know perfectly well how . . . as crinkly as yours . . . that's how.

Asagai   And it is ugly to you that way?

Beneatha (*quickly*)   Oh, no – not ugly . . . (*More slowly, apologetically.*) But it's so hard to manage when it's, well – raw.

Asagai   And so to accommodate that – you mutilate it every week?

Beneatha   It's not mutilation!

Asagai (*laughing aloud at her seriousness*)   Oh . . . please! I am only teasing you because you are so very serious about these things. (*He stands back from her and folds his arms across his chest as he watches her pulling at her hair and frowning in the mirror.*) Do you remember the first time you met me at school? . . . (*He laughs.*) You came up to me and you said – and I thought you were the most serious little thing I had ever seen – you said: (*he imitates her*) 'Mr. Asagai – I want very much to talk with you. About Africa. You see, Mr. Asagai, I am looking for my *identity!* (*He laughs.*)

Beneatha (*turning to him, not laughing*)   Yes – (*Her face is quizzical, profoundly disturbed.*)

Asagai (*still teasing and reaching out and taking her face in his hands and turning her profile to him*)   Well . . . it is true that this is not so much a profile of a Hollywood queen as perhaps a queen of the Nile – (*A mock dismissal of the importance of the question.*) But what does it matter? Assimilationism is so popular in your country.

Beneatha (*wheeling, passionately, sharply*)   I am not an assimilationist!

Asagai (*the protest hangs in the room for a moment and* **Asagai** *studies her, his laughter fading*)   Such a serious one. (*There is a pause.*) So – you like the robes? You must take excellent care of them – they are from my sister's personal wardrobe.

Beneatha (*with incredulity*)   You – you sent all the way home – for me?

Asagai (*with charm*)   For you – I would do much more . . . Well, that is what I came for. I must go.

Beneatha   Will you call me Monday?

Asagai   Yes . . . We have a great deal to talk about. I mean about identity and time and all that.

Beneatha   Time?

Asagai   Yes. About how much time one needs to know what one feels.

Beneatha   You never understood that there is more than one kind of feeling which can exist between a man and a woman – or, at least, there should be.

Asagai (*shaking his head negatively but gently*)   No. Between a man and a woman there need be only one kind of feeling. I have that for you . . . Now even . . . right this moment . . .

Beneatha I know – and by itself – it won't do. I can find that anywhere.

Asagai For a woman it should be enough.

Beneatha I know – because that's what it says in all the novels that men write. But it isn't. Go ahead and laugh – but I'm not interested in being someone's little episode in America or (*with feminine vengeance*) one of them! (**Asagai** *has burst into laughter again.*) That's funny as hell, huh!

Asagai It's just that every American girl I have known has said that to me. White – black – in this you are all the same. And the same speech, too!

Beneatha (*angrily*) Yuk, yuk, yuk!

Asagai It's how you can be sure that the world's most liberated women are not liberated at all. You all talk about it too much!

Mama *enters and is immediately all social charm because of the presence of a guest.*

Beneatha Oh – Mama – this is Mr. Asagai.

Mama How do you do?

Asagai (*total politeness to an elder*) How do you do, Mrs. Younger. Please forgive me for coming at such an outrageous hour on a Saturday.

Mama Well, you are quite welcome. I just hope you understand that our house don't always look like this. (*Chatterish.*) You must come again. I would love to hear all about (*not sure of the name*) your country. I think it's so sad the way our American Negroes don't know nothing about Africa 'cept Tarzan and all that. And all that money they pour into these churches when they ought to be helping you people over there drive out them French and Englishmen done taken away your land.

The mother flashes a slightly superior look at her daughter upon completion of the recitation.

Asagai (*taken aback by this sudden and acutely unrelated expression of sympathy*)   Yes . . . yes . . .

Mama (*smiling at him suddenly and relaxing and looking him over*) How many miles is it from here to where you come from?

Asagai   Many thousands.

Mama (*looking at him as she would* **Walter**)   I bet you don't half look after yourself, being away from your mama either. I spec you better come 'round here from time to time and get yourself some decent home-cooked meals . . .

Asagai (*moved*)   Thank you. Thank you very much. (*They are all quiet, then*) Well . . . I must go. I will call you Monday, Alaiyo.

Mama   What's that he call you?

Asagai   Oh – 'Alaiyo'. I hope you don't mind. It is what you would call a nickname, I think. It is a Yoruba word. I am a Yoruba.

Mama (*looking at* **Beneatha**)   I – I thought he was from –

Asagai (*understanding*)   Nigeria is my country. Yoruba is my tribal origin –

Beneatha   You didn't tell us what Alaiyo means . . . for all I know, you might be calling me Little Idiot or something . . .

Asagai   Well . . . let me see . . . I do not know how just to explain it . . . The sense of a thing can be so different when it changes languages.

Beneatha   You're evading.

Asagai   No – really it is difficult . . . (*Thinking.*) It means . . . it means One for Whom Bread – Food – Is Not Enough. (*He looks at her.*) Is that all right?

Beneatha (*understanding, softly*)   Thank you.

Mama (*looking from one to the other and not understanding any of it*) Well . . . that's nice . . . You must come see us again – Mr. –

Asagai   Ah-sah-guy . . .

Mama   Yes . . . Do come again.

Asagai   Good-bye.

He goes.

Mama (*after him*)   Lord, that's a pretty thing just went out here! (*Insinuatingly, to her daughter.*) Yes, I guess I see why we done commence to get so interested in Africa 'round here. Missionaries my aunt Jenny!

She goes.

Beneatha   Oh, Mama! . . .

She picks up the Nigerian dress and holds it up to her in front of the mirror again. She sets the headdress on haphazardly and then notices her hair again and clutches at it and then replaces the headdress and frowns at herself. Then she starts to wriggle in front of the mirror as she thinks a Nigerian woman might. **Travis** *enters and regards her.*

Travis   You cracking up?

Beneatha   Shut up.

She pulls the headdress off and looks at herself in the mirror and clutches at her hair again and squinches her eyes as if trying to imagine something. Then, suddenly, she gets her raincoat and handkerchief and hurriedly prepares for going out.

Mama (*coming back into the room*)   She's resting now. Travis, baby, run next door and ask Miss Johnson to please let me have a little kitchen cleanser. This here can is empty as Jacob's kettle.

Travis   I just came in.

Mama   Do as you told. (*He goes and she looks at her daughter.*) Where you going?

Beneatha (*halting at the door*)   To become a queen of the Nile!

She goes in a breathless blaze of glory. **Ruth** *appears in the bedroom doorway.*

Mama   Who told you to get up?

Ruth   Ain't nothing wrong with me to be lying in no bed for. Where did Bennie go?

Mama (*drumming her fingers*)   Far as I could make out – to Egypt. (**Ruth** *just looks at her.*) What time is it getting to?

Ruth   Ten twenty. And that mailman going to ring that bell this morning just like he done every morning for the last umpteen years.

Travis *comes in with the cleanser can.*

Travis   She say to tell that she don't have much.

Mama (*angrily*)   Lord, some people I could name sure is tight-fisted! (*Directing her grandson*) Mark two cans of cleanser down on the list there. If she that hard up for kitchen cleanser, I sure don't want to forget to get her none!

Ruth   Lena – maybe the woman is just short on cleanser . . .

Mama (*not listening*) . . . Much baking powder as she done borrowed from me all these years, she could of done gone into the baking business!

The bell sounds suddenly and sharply and all three are stunned – serious and silent – mid-speech. In spite of all the other conversations and distractions of the morning, this is what they have been waiting for, even **Travis**, *who looks helplessly from his mother to his grandmother.* **Ruth** *is the first to come to life again.*

Ruth (*to* **Travis**)   *Get down them steps, boy!*

Travis *snaps to life and flies out to get the mail.*

Mama (*her eyes wide, her hand to her breast*)   You mean it done really come?

Ruth (*excited*)   Oh, Miss Lena!

Mama (*collecting herself*)   Well . . . I don't know what we all so excited about 'round here for. We known it was coming for months.

Ruth   That's a whole lot different from having it come and being able to hold it in your hands . . . a piece of paper worth ten thousand dollars . . . (**Travis** *bursts back into the room. He holds the envelope high above his head, like a little dancer, his face is radiant and he is breathless. He moves to his grandmother with sudden slow ceremony and puts the envelope into her hands. She accepts it, and then merely holds it and looks at it.*) Come on! Open it . . . Lord have mercy, I wish Walter Lee was here!

Travis   Open it, Grandmama!

Mama (*staring at it*)   Now you all be quiet. It's just a cheque.

Ruth   Open it . . .

Mama (*still staring at it*)   Now don't act silly . . . We ain't never been no people to act silly 'bout no money . . .

Ruth (*swiftly*)   We ain't never had none before – *open it!*

Mama *finally makes a good strong tear and pulls out the thin blue slice of paper and inspects it closely. The boy and his mother study it raptly over* **Mama**'s *shoulders.*

Mama   Travis! (*She is counting off with doubt.*) Is that the right number of zeros?

Travis   Yes'm . . . ten thousand dollars. Gaalee, Grandmama, you rich.

Mama (*she holds the cheque away from her, still looking at it. Slowly her face sobers into a mask of happiness*)   Ten thousand dollars. (*She hands it to* **Ruth**.) Put it away somewhere, Ruth. (*She does*

not look at **Ruth**; *her eyes seem to be seeing something very far off.*)
Ten thousand dollars they give you. Ten thousand dollars.

Travis (*to his mother, sincerely*)   What's the matter with
Grandmama – don't she want to be rich?

Ruth (*distractedly*)   You go on out and play now, baby.
(**Travis** *goes.* **Mama** *starts wiping dishes absently, humming
intently to herself.* **Ruth** *turns to her, with kind exasperation.*)
You've gone and got yourself upset.

Mama (*not looking at her*)   I spec if it wasn't for you all . . . I
would just put that money away or give it to the church or
something.

Ruth   Now what kind of talk is that. Mr. Younger would
just be plain mad if he could hear you talking foolish like
that.

Mama (*stopping and staring off*)   Yes . . . he sure would.
(*Sighing.*) We got enough to do with that money, all right.
(*She halts then, and turns and looks at her daughter-in-law hard;*
Ruth *avoids her eyes and* **Mama** *wipes her hands with finality and
starts to speak firmly to* **Ruth**) Where did you go today, girl?

Ruth   To the doctor.

Mama (*impatiently*)   Now, Ruth . . . you know better than
that. Old Doctor Jones is strange enough in his way but
there ain't nothing 'bout him make somebody slip and call
him 'she' – like you done this morning.

Ruth   Well, that's what happened – my tongue slipped.

Mama   You went to see that woman, didn't you?

Ruth (*defensively, giving herself away*)   What woman you
talking about?

Mama (*angrily*)   That woman who –

Walter *enters in great excitement.*

Walter   Did it come?

Mama (*quietly*)   Can you give people a Christian greeting before you start asking about money?

Walter (*to* **Ruth**)   Did it come? (**Ruth** *unfolds the cheque and lays it quietly before him, watching him intently with thoughts of her own.* **Walter** *sits down and grasps it close and counts off the zeros.*) Ten thousand dollars – (*He turns suddenly, frantically to his mother and draws some papers out of his breast pocket.*) Mama – look. Old Willy Harris put everything on paper –

Mama   Son – I think you ought to talk to your wife . . . I'll go on out and leave you alone if you want –

Walter   I can talk to her later – Mama, look –

Mama   Son –

Walter   WILL SOMEBODY PLEASE LISTEN TO ME TODAY!

Mama (*quietly*)   I don't 'low no yellin' in this house, Walter Lee, and you know it – (**Walter** *stares at them in frustration and starts to speak several times.*) And there ain't going to be no investing in no liquor stores. I don't aim to have to speak on that again.

A long pause.

Walter   Oh – so you don't aim to have to speak on that again? So *you* have decided . . . (*Crumpling his papers.*) Well, *you* tell that to my boy tonight when you put him to sleep on the living-room couch . . . (*Turning to* **Mama** *and speaking directly to her.*) Yeah – and tell it to my wife, Mama, tomorrow when she has to go out of here to look after somebody else's kids. And tell it to *me*, Mama, every time we need a new pair of curtains and I have to watch *you* go out and work in somebody's kitchen. Yeah, you tell me then!

Walter *starts to go.*

Ruth   Where you going?

Walter   I'm going out!

Ruth   Where?

Walter   Just out of this house somewhere –

Ruth (*getting her coat*)   I'll come too.

Walter   I don't want you to come!

Ruth   I got something to talk to you about, Walter.

Walter   That's too bad.

Mama (*still quietly*)   Walter Lee – (*She waits and he finally turns and looks at her.*) Sit down.

Walter   I'm a grown man, Mama.

Mama   Ain't nobody said you wasn't grown. But you still in my house and my presence. And as long as you are – you'll talk to your wife civil. Now sit down.

Ruth (*suddenly*)   Oh, let him go on out and drink himself to death! He makes me sick to my stomach! (*She flings her coat against him.*)

Walter (*violently*)   And you turn mine too, baby! (**Ruth** *goes into their bedroom and slams the door behind her.*) That was my greatest mistake –

Mama (*still quietly*)   Walter, what is the matter with you?

Walter   Matter with me? Ain't nothing the matter with *me!*

Mama   Yes there is. Something eating you up like a crazy man. Something more than me not giving you this money. The past few years I been watching it happen to you. You get all nervous acting and kind of wild in the eyes – (**Walter** *jumps up impatiently at her words.*) I said sit there now, I'm talking to you!

Walter   Mama – I don't need no nagging at me today.

Mama   Seem like you getting to a place where you always tied up in some kind of knot about something. But if anybody ask you 'bout it you just yell at 'em and bust out the house and go out and drink somewheres. Walter Lee, people can't live with that. Ruth's a good, patient girl in her way – but you getting to be too much. Boy, don't make the mistake of driving that girl away from you.

Walter   Why – what she do for me?

Mama   She loves you.

Walter   Mama – I'm going out. I want to go off somewhere and be by myself for a while.

Mama   I'm sorry 'bout your liquor store, son. It just wasn't the thing for us to do. That's what I want to tell you about –

Walter   I got to go out, Mama – (*He rises.*)

Mama   It's dangerous, son.

Walter   What's dangerous?

Mama   When a man goes outside his home to look for peace.

Walter (*beseechingly*)   Then why can't there never be no peace in this house then?

Mama   You done found it in some other house?

Walter   No – there ain't no woman! Why do women always think there's a woman somewhere when a man gets restless. (*Coming to her.*) Mama – Mama – I want so many things . . .

Mama   Yes, son –

Walter   I want so many things that they are driving me kind of crazy . . . Mama – look at me.

Mama   I'm looking at you. You a good-looking boy. You got a job, a nice wife, a fine boy and –

Walter   A job. (*Looks at her.*) Mama, a job? I open and close car doors all day long. I drive a man around in his limousine and I say, 'Yes, sir; no sir; very good, sir; shall I take the Drive, sir?' Mama, that ain't no kind of job . . . that ain't nothing at all. (*Very quietly*.) Mama, I don't know if I can make you understand.

Mama   Understand what, baby?

Walter (*quietly*)   Sometimes it's like I can see the future stretched out in front of me – just plain as day. The future, Mama. Hanging over there at the edge of my days. Just waiting for me – a big, looming blank space – full of *nothing*. Just waiting for *me*. (*Pause*.) Mama – sometimes when I'm downtown and I pass them cool, quiet-looking restaurants where them white boys are sitting back and talking 'bout things . . . sitting there turning deals worth millions of dollars . . . sometimes I see guys don't look much older than me –

Mama   Son – how come you talk so much 'bout money?

Walter (*with immense passion*)   Because it is life, Mama!

Mama (*quietly*)   Oh – (*Very quietly*.)   So now it's life. Money is life. Once upon a time freedom used to be life – now it's money. I guess the world really do change . . .

Walter   No – it was always money, Mama. We just didn't know about it.

Mama   No . . . something has changed. (*She looks at him*.) You something new, boy. In my time we was worried about not being lynched and getting to the North if we could and how to stay alive and still have a pinch of dignity too . . . Now here come you and Beneatha – talking 'bout things we ain't never even thought about hardly, me and your daddy. You ain't satisfied or proud of nothing we done. I mean that you had a home; that we kept you out of trouble till you was grown; that you don't have to ride to work on the back of nobody's streetcar – You my children – but how different we done become.

Walter   You just don't understand, Mama, you just don't understand.

Mama   Son – do you know your wife is expecting another baby? (**Walter** *stands, stunned, and absorbs what his mother has said.*) That's what she wanted to talk to you about. (**Walter** *sinks down into a chair.*) This ain't for me to be telling – but you ought to know. (*She waits.*) I think Ruth is thinking 'bout getting rid of that child.

Walter (*slowly understanding*)   No – no – Ruth wouldn't do that.

Mama   When the world gets ugly enough – a woman will do anything for her family. *The part that's already living.*

Walter   You don't know Ruth, Mama, if you think she would do that.

Ruth *opens the bedroom door and stands there a little limp.*

Ruth (*beaten*)   Yes I would too, Walter. (*Pause.*) I gave her a five-dollar down payment.

There is total silence as the man stares at his wife and the mother stares at her son.

Mama (*presently*)   Well – (*Tightly.*) Well – son, I'm waiting to hear you say something . . . I'm waiting to hear how you be your father's son. Be the man he was . . . (*Pause.*) Your wife say she going to destroy your child. And I'm waiting to hear you talk like him and say we a people who give children life, not who destroys them – (*She rises.*) I'm waiting to see you stand up and look like your daddy and say we done give up one baby to poverty and that we ain't going to give up nary another one . . . I'm waiting.

Walter   Ruth –

Mama   If you a son of mine, tell her! (**Walter** *turns, looks at her and can say nothing. She continues, bitterly.*) You . . . you are a disgrace to your father's memory. Somebody get me my hat.

Curtain.

Act Two

Scene One

Time: Later the same day.

At rise: **Ruth** *is ironing again. She has the radio going. Presently* **Beneatha**'s *bedroom door opens and* **Ruth**'s *mouth falls and she puts down the iron in fascination.*

Ruth   What have we got on tonight?

Beneatha (*emerging grandly from the doorway so that we can see her thoroughly robed in the costume* **Asagai** *brought*)   You are looking at what a well-dressed Nigerian woman wears. (*She parades for* **Ruth**, *her hair completely hidden by the headdress; she is coquettishly fanning herself with an ornate oriental fan, mistakenly more like Butterfly than any Nigerian that ever was.*) Isn't it beautiful? (*She promenades to the radio and, with an arrogant flourish, turns off the good loud blues that is playing.*) Enough of this assimilationist junk! (**Ruth** *follows her with her eyes as she goes to the gramophone and puts on a record and turns and waits ceremoniously for the music to come up. Then, with a shout*) OCOMOGOSIAY!

Ruth *jumps. The music comes up, a lovely Nigerian melody.* **Beneatha** *listens, enraptured, her eyes far away – 'back to the past'. She begins to dance.* **Ruth** *is dumbfounded.*

Ruth   What kind of dance is that?

Beneatha   A folk dance.

Ruth (*as Pearl Bailey*)   What kind of folks do that, honey?

Beneatha   It's from Nigeria. It's a dance of welcome.

Ruth   Who you welcoming?

Beneatha   The men back to the village.

Ruth   Where they been?

Beneatha   How should I know – out hunting or
something. Anyway, they are coming back now . . .

Ruth   Well, that's good.

Beneatha (*with the record*)

Alundi, alundi
Alundi alunya
Jop pu a jeepua
Ang gu soooooooooo
Ai yai yae . . .
Ayehaye – alundi . . .

Walter *comes in during this performance; he has obviously been
drinking. He leans against the door heavily and watches his sister, at
first with distaste. Then his eyes look off – 'back to the past' – as he
lifts both his fists to the roof, screaming.*

Walter   YEAH . . . AND ETHIOPIA STRETCH FORTH HER
HANDS AGAIN! . . .

Ruth (*drily, looking at him*)   Yes – and Africa sure is claiming
her own tonight. (*She gives them both up and starts ironing again.*)

Walter (*all in a drunken, dramatic shout*)   Shut up! . . . I'm
digging them drums . . . them drums move me! . . . (*He makes
his weaving way to his wife's face and leans in close to her.*) In my
heart of hearts (*he thumps his chest*) I am much warrior!

Ruth (*without even looking up*)   In your heart of hearts you
are much drunkard.

Walter (*coming away from her and starting to wander around the
room, shouting*)   Me and Jomo . . . (*Intently, in his sister's
face. She has stopped dancing to watch him in this unknown mood.*)
That's my man, Kenyatta. (*Shouting and thumping his chest.*)
FLAMING SPEAR! HOT DAMN! (*He is suddenly in possession of
an imaginary spear and actively spearing enemies all over the room.*)
OCOMOGOSIAY . . . THE LION IS WAKING . . . OWIMOWEH!
(*He pulls his shirt open and leaps up on a table and gestures with his
spear. The bell rings.* **Ruth** *goes to answer.*)

Beneatha (*to encourage* **Walter**, *thoroughly caught up with this side of him*)   OCOMOGOSIAY, FLAMING SPEAR!

Walter (*on the table, very far gone, his eyes pure glass sheets. He sees what we cannot, that he is a leader of his people, a great chief, a descendant of Chaka, and that the hour to March has come*)   Listen, my black brothers –

Beneatha   OCOMOGOSIAY!

Walter   . . . Do you hear the waters rushing against the shores of the coastlands –

Beneatha   OCOMOGOSIAY!

Walter   . . . Do you hear the screeching of the cocks in yonder hills beyond where the chiefs meet in council for the coming of the mighty war –

Beneatha   OCOMOGOSIAY!

Walter   . . . Do you hear the beating of the wings of the birds flying low over the mountains and the low places of our land –

Ruth *opens the door.* **George Murchison** *enters.*

Beneatha   OCOMOGOSIAY!

Walter   . . . Do you hear the singing of the women, singing the war songs of our fathers to the babies in the great houses . . . singing the sweet war songs? OH, DO YOU HEAR, MY BLACK BROTHERS!

Beneatha (*completely gone*)   We hear you, Flaming Spear –

Walter   Telling us to prepare for the greatness of the time – (*To* **George.**) Black Brother! (*He extends his hand for the fraternal clasp.*)

George   Black Brother, hell!

Ruth (*having had enough, and embarrassed for the family*) Beneatha, you got company – what's the matter with you?

Walter Lee Younger, get down off that table and stop acting like a fool . . .

Walter *comes down off the table suddenly and makes a quick exit to the bathroom.*

Ruth   He's had a little to drink . . . I don't know what her excuse is.

George (*to* **Beneatha**)   Look honey, we're going *to* the theatre – we're not going to be *in* it . . . so go change, huh?

Ruth   You expect this boy to go out with you looking like that?

Beneatha *looks at him and slowly, ceremoniously, lifts her hands and pulls off the head-dress. Her hair is close-cropped and unstraightened.* **George** *freezes mid-sentence and* **Ruth***'s eyes all but fall out of her head.*

George   What in the name of –

Ruth (*touching* **Beneatha***'s hair*)   Girl, you done lost your natural mind!? Look at your head!

George   What have you done to your head – I mean your hair?

Beneatha   Nothing – except cut it off.

Ruth   You expect this boy to go out with you looking like that?!

Beneatha (*looking at* **George**)   That's up to George. If he's ashamed of his heritage –

George   Oh, don't be so proud of yourself, Bennie – just because you look eccentric.

Beneatha   How can something that's natural be eccentric?

George   That's what being eccentric means – being natural. Get dressed.

Beneatha   I don't like that, George.

Ruth   Why must you and your brother make an argument out of everything people say?

Beneatha   Because I hate assimilationist Negroes!

Ruth   Will somebody please tell me what assimila-whoever means!

George   Oh, it's just a college girl's way of calling people Uncle Toms. But that isn't what it means at all.

Ruth   Well, what does it mean?

Beneatha (*cutting* **George** *off and staring at him as she replies to* **Ruth**)   It means someone who is willing to give up his own culture and submerge himself completely in the dominant, and in this case, *oppressive*, culture!

George   Oh, dear, dear, dear! Here we go! A lecture on the African past! On our Great West African Heritage! In one second we will hear all about the great Ashanti empires, the great Songhay civilisations and the great sculpture of Bénin – and then some poetry in the Bantu – and the whole monologue will end with the work *heritage*! (*Nastily.*) Let's face it, baby, your heritage is nothing but a bunch of raggedy-assed spirituals and some grass huts!

Beneatha   *Grass huts*!

Ruth *crosses to her and forcibly pushes her toward the bedroom.*

See there . . . You are standing there in your splendid ignorance talking about people who were the first to smelt iron on the face of the earth!

Ruth *is pushing her through the door.*

The Ashanti were performing surgical operations when the English –

Ruth *pulls the door to, with* **Beneatha** *on the other side, and smiles graciously at* **George**. **Beneatha** *opens the door and shouts the end of the sentence defiantly at* **George**.

– were still tattooing themselves with blue dragons . . . (*She goes back inside.*)

Ruth   Have a seat, George.

They both sit. **Ruth** *folds her hands rather primly on her lap, determined to demonstrate the civilisation of the family.*

Warm, ain't it? I mean for September. (*Pause.*) Just like they always say about Chicago weather: If it's too hot or cold for you, just wait a minute and it'll change. (*She smiles happily at this cliché of clichés.*) Everybody say it's got to do with them bombs and things they keep setting off. (*Pause.*) Would you like a nice cold beer?

George   No, thank you. I don't care for beer. (*He looks at his watch.*) I hope she hurries up.

Ruth   What time is the show?

George   It's an eight-thirty curtain. That's just Chicago, though. In New York standard curtain time is eight forty. (*He is rather proud of this knowledge.*)

Ruth (*properly appreciating it*)   You get to New York a lot?

George (*offhand*)   Few times a year.

Ruth   Oh – that's nice. I've never been to New York.

Walter *enters. We feel the edge of unreality is still with him.*

Walter   New York ain't got nothing Chicago ain't. Just a bunch of hustling people all squeezed up together – being 'Eastern'. (*He turns his face into a screw of displeasure.*)

George   Oh – you've been?

Walter   *Plenty* of times.

Ruth (*shocked at the lie*)   Walter Lee Younger!

Walter (*staring her down*)   Plenty! (*Pause.*) What we got to drink in this house? Why don't you offer this man some refreshment. (*To* **George**.) They don't know how to entertain people in this house, man.

George   Thank you – I don't really care for anything.

Walter (*feeling his head, sobriety coming*)   Where's Mama?

Ruth   She ain't come back yet.

Walter (*Looking* **George** *over from head to toe, scrutinising his carefully casual tweed sports jacket over cashmere V-neck sweater over soft eyelet shirt and tie, and soft slacks, finished off with white buckskin shoes*)   Why all you college boys wear them faggoty-looking white shoes?

Ruth   Walter Lee!

George *ignores the remark.*

Walter (*to* **Ruth**)   Well, they look crazy as hell – white shoes, cold as it is.

Ruth (*crushed*)   You have to excuse him –

Walter   No, he don't! Excuse me for what? What you always excusing me for! I'll excuse myself when I needs to be excused! (*Pause.*) They look as funny as them black knee socks Beneatha wears out of here all the time.

Ruth   It's the college *style*, Walter.

Walter   Style, hell. She looks like she got burnt legs or something!

Ruth   Oh, Walter –

Walter (*an irritable mimic*)   Oh, Walter! Oh, Walter! (*to* **George**.) How's your old man making out? I understand you all going to buy that big hotel on the Drive? (*He finds a beer in the refrigerator, wanders over to* **George**, *sipping and wiping his lips with the back of his hand and straddling a chair backwards to talk to the other man.*) Shrewd move. Your old man is all right, man. (*Tapping his head and half winking for emphasis.*) I mean he knows how to operate. I mean he thinks *big*, you know what I mean, I mean for a *home*, you know? But I think he's kind of running out of ideas now. I'd like to talk to him. Listen, man, I got some plans that could turn this city upside down.

I mean I think like he does. *Big.* Invest big, gamble big, hell, lose *big* if you have to, you know what I mean. It's hard to find a man on this whole Southside who understands my kind of thinking – you dig? (*He scrutinises* **George** *again, drinks his beer, squints his eyes and leans in close, confidential, man to man.*) Me and you ought to sit down and talk sometimes, man. Man, I got me some ideas . . .

George (*with boredom*)   Yeah – sometimes we'll have to do that, Walter.

Walter (*understanding the indifference, and offended*)   Yeah – well, when you get the time, man. I know you a busy little boy.

Ruth   Walter, please –

Walter (*bitterly, hurt*)   I know ain't nothing in this world as busy as you coloured college boys with your fraternity pins and white shoes . . .

Ruth (*covering her face with humiliation*)   Oh, Walter Lee –

Walter   I see you all all the time – with the books tucked under your arms – going to your – (*He mimics the British* 'a'.) 'clahsses'. And for what? What the hell you learning over there? Filling up your heads – (*Counting off on his fingers.*) – with the sociology and the psychology. But they teaching you how to be a man? How to take over and run the world? They teaching you how to run a rubber plantation or a steel mill? Naw – just to talk proper and read books and wear them faggoty-looking white shoes . . .

George (*looking at him with distaste, a little above it all*)   You're all whacked up with bitterness, man.

Walter (*intently, almost quietly, between the teeth, glaring at the boy*)   And you – ain't you bitter, man? Ain't you just about had it yet? Don't you see no stars gleaming that you can't reach out and grab? You happy? – you contented son-of-a-bitch – you happy? You got it made? Bitter? Man, I'm a volcano. Bitter? Here I am a giant – surrounded by ants! Ants who can't even understand what it is the giant is talking about.

Ruth (*passionately and suddenly*)   Oh, Walter – ain't you with nobody?

Walter (*violently*)   No! 'Cause ain't nobody with me! Not even my own mother!

Ruth   Walter, that's a terrible thing to say!

Beneatha *enters, dressed for the evening in a cocktail dress and earrings, hair natural.*

George   Well, hey – (*Thoughtful, with emphasis, since this is a reversal.*) – you look great.

Walter (*seeing his sister's hair for the first time*)   – What's the matter with your head?

Beneatha (*tired of the jokes now*)   I cut it off, Brother.

Walter (*coming close to inspect it and walking around her*)   Well, I'll be damned. So that's what they mean by the African bush.

Beneatha   Let's go, George.

George   You know something? I like it. It's sharp. I mean, it really is. (*Helps her into her wrap.*)

Ruth   Yes, I think so too.

Walter   Oh no! You leave yours alone, baby. You might turn out to have a pin-shaped head or something!

Beneatha   See you all later.

Ruth   Have a nice time.

George   Thanks. Good night. (*To* **Walter.**) Good night, *Prometheus.*

Beneatha *and* **George** *exit.*

Walter (*to* **Ruth**)   Who is Prometheus?

Ruth   I don't know. Don't worry about it.

Walter (*in fury, pointing after* **George**) See there – they get to a point where they can't insult you man to man – they got to go talk about something ain't nobody never heard of!

Ruth How you know it was an insult! (*To humour him.*) Maybe Prometheus is a nice fellow.

Walter Prometheus! I bet there ain't even no such thing! I bet that simple-minded clown –

Ruth Walter – (*She stops what she is doing and looks at him.*)

Walter (*yelling*) Don't start!

Ruth Start what?

Walter Your nagging! Where was I? Who was I with? How much money did I spend?

Ruth (*plaintively*) Walter Lee – why don't we just try to talk about it . . .

Walter (*not listening*) I been out talking with people who understand me. People who care about the things I got on my mind.

Ruth (*wearily*) I guess that means people like Willy Harris.

Walter Yes, people like Willy Harris.

Ruth (*with a sudden flash of impatience*) Why don't you all just hurry up and go into the banking business and stop talking about it!

Walter Why? You want to know why? 'Cause we all tied up in a race of people that don't know how to do nothing but moan, pray and have babies!

The line is too bitter even for him and he looks at her and sits down.

Ruth Oh, Walter . . . (*Softly.*) Honey, why can't you stop fighting me?

Walter (*without thinking*) Who's fighting you? Who even cares about you?

This line begins the retardation of his mood.

Ruth   Well – (*She waits a long time, and then with resignation starts to put away her things.*) I guess I might as well go on to bed . . . (*More or less to herself.*) I don't know where we lost it . . . but we have . . . (*Then, to him.*) I – I'm sorry about this new baby, Walter. I guess maybe I better go on and do what I started . . . I guess I just didn't realize how bad things was with us . . . I guess I just didn't really realize – (*She starts out to the bedroom and stops.*) You want some hot milk?

Walter   Hot milk?

Ruth   Yes – hot milk.

Walter   Why hot milk?

Ruth   'Cause after all that liquor you come home with you ought to have something hot in your stomach.

Walter   I don't want no milk.

Ruth   You want some coffee then?

Walter   No, I don't want no coffee. I don't want nothing hot to drink. (*Almost plaintively.*) Why you always trying to give me something to eat?

Ruth (*standing and looking at him helplessly*)   What else can I give you, Walter Lee Younger?

She stands and looks at him and presently turns to go out again. He lifts his head and watches her going away from him in a new mood which began to emerge when he asked her 'Who cares about you?'

Walter   It's been rough, ain't it, baby? (*She hears and stops but does not turn round as he continues to her back.*) I guess between two people there ain't never as much understood as folks generally thinks there is. I mean like between me and you – (*She turns to face him.*) How we gets to the place where we scared to talk softness to each other. (*He waits, thinking hard himself.*) Why you think it got to be like that? (*He is thoughtful, almost as a child would be.*) Ruth, what is it gets into people ought to be close?

Ruth   I don't know, honey. I think about it a lot.

Walter   On account of you and me, you mean? The way things are with us. The way something done come down between us.

Ruth   There ain't so much between us, Walter . . . Not when you come to me and try to talk to me. Try to be with me . . . a little even.

Walter (*total honesty*)   Sometimes . . . sometimes . . . I don't even know how to try.

Ruth   Walter –

Walter   Yes?

Ruth (*coming to him, gently and with misgiving, but coming to him*) Honey . . . life don't have to be like this. I mean sometimes people can do things so that things are better . . . You remember how we used to talk when Travis was born . . . about the way we were going to live . . . the kind of house . . . (*She is stroking his head.*) Well, it's all starting to slip away from us . . .

Mama *enters, and* **Walter** *jumps up and shouts at her.*

Walter   Mama, where have you been?

Mama   My – them steps is longer than they used to be. Whew! (*She sits down and ignores him.*) How you feeling this evening, Ruth?

Ruth *shrugs, disturbed some at having been prematurely interrupted and watching her husband knowingly.*

Walter   Mama, where have you been all day?

Mama (*still ignoring him and leaning on the table and changing to more comfortable shoes*).   Where's Travis?

Ruth   I let him go out earlier and he ain't come back yet. Boy, is he going to get it!

Walter   Mama!

Mama (*as if she has heard him for the first time*)   Yes, son?

Walter   Where did you go this afternoon?

Mama   I went down town to tend to some business that I had to tend to.

Walter   What kind of business?

Mama   You know better than to question me like a child, Brother.

Walter (*rising and bending over the table*)   Where were you, Mama? (*Bringing his fists down and shouting.*) Mama, you didn't go do something with that insurance money, something crazy?

The front door opens slowly, interrupting him, and **Travis** *pokes his head in, less than hopefully.*

Travis (*to his mother*)   Mama, I –

Ruth   'Mama I' nothing! You're going to get it, boy! Get on in that bedroom and get yourself ready!

Travis   But I –

Mama   Why don't you all never let the child explain hisself.

Ruth   Keep out of it now, Lena.

Mama *clamps her lips together, and* **Ruth** *advances towards her son menacingly.*

Ruth   A thousand times I have told you not to go off like that –

Mama (*holding out her arms to her grandson*)   Well – at least let me tell him something. I want him to be the first one to hear . . . Come here, Travis. (*The boy obeys gladly.*) Travis (*she takes him by the shoulders and looks into his face*) you know that money we got in the mail this morning?

Travis   Yes'm –

Mama   Well – what you think your grandmama gone and done with that money?

Travis   I don't know, Grandmama.

Mama (*putting her finger on his nose for emphasis*)   She went out and she bought you a house! (*The explosion comes from* **Walter** *at the end of the revelation and he jumps up and turns away from all of them in a fury.* **Mama** *continues, to* **Travis**.) You glad about the house? It's going to be yours when you get to be a man.

Travis   Yeah – I always wanted to live in a house.

Mama   All right, gimme some sugar then. (**Travis** *puts his arms around her neck as she watches her son over the boy's shoulder. Then, to* **Travis**, *after the embrace.*) Now when you say your prayers tonight, you thank God and your grandfather – 'cause it was him who give you the house – in his way.

Ruth (*taking the boy from* **Mama** *and pushing him towards the bedroom*)   Now you get out of here and get ready for your beating.

Travis   Aw, Mama –

Ruth   Get on in there. (*Closing the door behind him and turning radiantly to her mother-in-law.*) So you went and did it!

Mama (*quietly, looking at her son with pain*)   Yes, I did.

Ruth (*raising both arms classically*)   Praise God! (*Looks at* **Walter** *a moment, who says nothing. She crosses rapidly to her husband.*) Please, honey – let me be glad . . . you be glad too. (*She has laid her hands on his shoulders, but he shakes himself free of her roughly, without turning to face her.*) Oh, Walter . . . a home . . . a home. (*She comes back to* **Mama**.) Well – where is it? How big is it? How much it going to cost?

Mama   Well –

Ruth   When we moving?

Mama (*smiling at her*)   First of the month.

Ruth (*throwing back her head with jubilance*)   Praise God!

Mama (*tentatively, still looking at her son's back turned against her and* **Ruth**)   It's – it's a nice house too . . . (*She cannot help speaking directly to him. An imploring quality in her voice, her manner, makes her almost like a girl now.*) Three bedrooms – nice big one for you and Ruth . . . Me and Beneatha still have to share our room, but Travis have one of his own – and – (*with difficulty*) I figures if the – new baby – is a boy, we could get one of them double-decker outfits . . . And there's yard with a little patch of dirt where I could maybe get to grow me a few flowers . . . And a nice big basement . . .

Ruth   Walter honey, be glad –

Mama (*still to his back, fingering things on the table*)   'Course I don't want to make it sound fancier than it is . . . it's just a plain little old house – but it's made good and solid – and it will be *ours*. Walter Lee – it makes a difference in a man when he can walk on floors that belong to *him* . . .

Ruth   Where is it?

Mama (*frightened at this telling*)   Well – well – it's out there in Clybourne Park –

Ruth's *radiance fades abruptly, and* **Walter** *finally turns slowly to face his mother with incredulity and hostility.*

Ruth   Where?

Mama (*matter-of-factly*)   Four o six Clybourne Street, Clybourne Park.

Ruth   Clybourne Park? Mama, there ain't no coloured people living in Clybourne Park.

Mama (*almost idiotically*)   Well, I guess there's going to be some now.

Walter (*bitterly*)   So that's the peace and comfort you went out and bought for us today!

Mama (*raising her eyes to meet his finally*)   Son – I just tried to find the nicest place for the least amount of money for my family.

Ruth (*trying to recover from the shock*)   Well – well – 'course I ain't one never been 'fraid of no crackers, mind you – but – well, wasn't there no other houses nowhere?

Mama   Them houses they put up for coloured in them areas way out all seen to cost twice as much as other houses. I did the best I could.

Ruth (*struck senseless with the news, in its various degrees of goodness and trouble, she sits for a moment, her fists propping her chin in thought, and then she starts to rise, bringing her fists down with vigour, the radiance spreading from cheek to cheek again*)   Well – well! All I can say is – if this is my time in life – *my time* – to say good-bye – (*and she builds with momentum as she starts to circle the room with an exuberant, almost tearfully happy release*) – to these God-damned cracking walls! – (*she pounds the walls*) – and these marching roaches! – (*she wipes at an imaginary army of marching roaches*) – and this cramped little closet which ain't now or never was no kitchen . . . then I say it loud and good, *Hallelujah! And good-bye misery . . . I don't never want to see your ugly face again!* (*She laughs joyously, having practically destroyed the apartment, and flings her arms up and lets them come down happily, slowly, reflectively, over her abdomen, aware for the first time perhaps that the life therein pulses with happiness and not despair.*) Lena?

Mama (*moved, watching her happiness*)   Yes, honey?

Ruth (*looking off*)   Is there – is there a whole lot of sunlight?

Mama (*understanding*)   Yes child, there's a whole lot of sunlight.

Long pause.

Ruth   (*collecting herself and going to the door of the room* **Travis** *is in*)   Well – I guess I better see 'bout Travis. (*To* **Mama**.) Lord, I sure don't feel like whipping nobody today!

She goes.

Mama (*the mother and son are left alone now and the mother waits a long time, considering deeply, before she speaks*)   Son – you – you understand what I done, don't you? (**Walter** *is silent and* *sullen.*) I – I just seen my family falling apart today . . . just falling to pieces in front of my eyes . . . We couldn't of gone on like we was today. We was going backwards 'stead of forwards – talking 'bout killing babies and wishing each other was dead . . . When it gets like that in life – you just got to do something different, push on out and do something bigger . . . (*She waits.*) I wish you say something, son . . . I wish you'd say how deep inside you think I done the right thing –

Walter (*crossing slowly to his bedroom door and finally turning there and speaking measuredly*)   What you need me to say you done right for? *You* the head of this family. You run our lives like you want to. It was your money and you did what you wanted with it. So what you need for me to say it was all right for? (*Bitterly, to hurt her as deeply as he knows is possible.*) So you butchered up a dream of mine – you – who always talking 'bout your children's dreams . . .

Mama   Walter Lee –

He just closes the door behind him. **Mama** *sits alone, thinking heavily.*

Curtain.

Scene Two

Time: Friday night. A few weeks later.

At rise: Packing crates mark the intention of the family to move. **Beneatha** *and* **George** *come in, presumably from an evening out again.*

George   O.K. . . . O.K., whatever you say . . . (*They both sit on the couch. He tries to kiss her. She moves away.*) Look, we've had a nice evening; let's not spoil it huh? . . .

He again turns her head and tries to nuzzle in and she turns away from him, not with distaste but with momentary lack of interest; in a mood to pursue what they were talking about.

Beneatha   I'm *trying* to talk to you.

George   We always talk.

Beneatha   Yes – and I love to talk.

George (*exasperated; rising*)   I know it and I don't mind it sometimes . . . I want you to cut it out, see – The moody stuff, I mean, I don't like it. You're a nice girl . . . all over. That's all you need, honey, forget the atmosphere. Guys aren't going to go for the atmosphere – they're going to go for what they see. Be glad for that. Drop the Garbo routine. It doesn't go with you. As for myself, I want a nice (*groping*) simple (*thoughtfully*) sophisticated girl . . . not a poet – O.K.?

She rebuffs him again and he starts to leave.

Beneatha   Why are you angry?

George   Because this is stupid! I don't go out with you to discuss the nature of 'quiet desperation' or to hear all about your thoughts – because the world will go on thinking what it thinks regardless –

Beneatha   Then why read books? Why go to school?

George (*with artificial patience, counting on his fingers*)   It's simple. You read books – to learn facts – to get grades – to pass the course – to get a degree. That's all – it has nothing to do with thoughts.

A long pause.

Beneatha   I see. (*A longer pause as she looks at him.*) Good night, George.

George *looks at her a little oddly, and starts to go. He meets* **Mama** *coming in.*

George   Oh – hello, Mrs. Younger.

Mama   Hello, George, how you feeling?

George   Fine – fine, how are you?

Mama   Oh, a little tired. You know them steps can get you after a day's work. You all have a nice time tonight?

George   Yes – a fine time. Well, good night.

Mama   Good night. (*He goes.* **Mama** *closes the door behind her.*) Hello, honey. What you sitting like that for?

Beneatha   I'm just sitting.

Mama   Didn't you have a nice time?

Beneatha   No.

Mama   No? What's the matter?

Beneatha   Mama, George is a fool – honest. (*She rises.*)

Mama (*hustling around unloading the packages she has entered with. She stops*)   Is he, baby?

Beneatha   Yes.

Beneatha *makes up* **Travis**'s *bed as she talks.*

Mama   You sure?

Beneatha   Yes.

Mama   Well – I guess you better not waste your time with no fools.

Beneatha *looks up at her mother, watching her put groceries in the refrigerator. Finally she gathers up her things and starts into the bedroom. At the door she stops and looks back at her mother.*

Beneatha   Mama –

Mama   Yes, baby –

Beneatha   Thank you.

Mama   For what?

Beneatha   For understanding me this time.

She goes out quickly and the mother stands, smiling a little, looking at the place where **Beneatha** *just stood.* **Ruth** *enters.*

Ruth Now don't you fool with any of this stuff, Lena –

Mama Oh, I just thought I'd sort a few things out.

The phone rings. **Ruth** *answers.*

Ruth (*at the phone*) Hello – just a minute. (*Goes to door.*) Walter, it's Mrs. Arnold. (*Waits. Goes back to the phone. Tense.*) Hello. Yes, this is his wife speaking . . . He's lying down now. Yes . . . well, he'll be in tomorrow. He's been very sick. Yes – I know we should have called, but we were so sure he'd be able to come in today. Yes – yes, I'm very sorry. Yes . . . Thank you very much. (*She hangs up.* **Walter** *is standing in the doorway of the bedroom behind her.*) That was Mrs. Arnold.

Walter (*indifferently*) Was it?

Ruth She said if you don't come in tomorrow that they are getting a new man . . .

Walter Ain't that sad – ain't that crying sad.

Ruth She said Mr. Arnold has had to take a cab for three days . . . Walter, you ain't been to work for three days! (*This is a revelation to her.*) Where you been, Walter Lee Younger? (**Walter** *looks at her and starts to laugh.*) You're going to lose your job.

Walter That's right . . .

Ruth Oh, Walter, and with your mother working like a dog every day –

Walter That's sad too. Everything is sad.

Mama What you been doing for these three days, son?

Walter Mama – you don't know all the things a man what got leisure can find to do in this city . . . What's this – Friday night? Well – Wednesday I borrowed Willy Harris's car and I went for a drive . . . just me and myself and I drove and drove . . . Way out . . . way past South Chicago, and I parked the car and I sat and looked at the steel mills all day long. I just sat in the car and looked at them big

black chimneys for hours. Then I drove back and I went to
the Green Hat. (*Pause.*) And Thursday – Thursday I
borrowed the car again and I got in it and I pointed it the
other way and I drove the other way – for hours – way, way
up to Wisconsin, and I looked at the farms. I just drove and
looked at the farms. Then I drove back and I went to the
Green Hat. (*Pause.*) And today – today I didn't get the car.
Today I just walked. All over the Southside. And I looked at
the Negroes and they looked at me and finally I just sat
down on the kerb at Thirty-ninth and South Parkway and I
just sat there and watched the Negroes go by. And then I
went to the Green Hat. You all sad? You all depressed? And
you know where I am going right now –

Ruth *goes out quietly.*

Mama   Oh, Big Walter, is this the harvest of our days?

Walter   You know what I like about the Green Hat? (*He
turns the radio on and a steamy, deep blues pours into the room.*) I like
this little cat they got there who blows a sax . . . He blows.
He talks to me. He ain't but 'bout five feet tall and he's got
a conked head and his eyes is always closed and he's all
music –

Mama (*rising and getting some papers out of her handbag*)
Walter –

Walter   And there's this other guy who plays the piano
. . . and they got a sound. I mean they can work on some
music . . . They got the best little combo in the world in the
Green Hat . . . You can just sit there and drink and listen to
them three men play and you realize that don't nothing
matter worth a damn, but just being there –

Mama   I've helped do it to you, haven't I, son? Walter, I
been wrong.

Walter   Naw – you ain't never been wrong about nothing,
Mama.

Mama   Listen to me, now. I say I been wrong, son. That I been doing to you what the rest of the world been doing to you. (*She stops and he looks up slowly at her and she meets his eyes pleadingly.*) Walter – what you ain't never understood is that I ain't got nothing, don't own nothing, ain't never really wanted nothing that wasn't for you. There ain't nothing as precious to me . . . There ain't nothing worth holding on to, money, dreams, nothing else – if it means – if it means it's going to destroy my boy. (*She puts her papers in front of him and he watches her without speaking or moving.*) I paid the man thirty-five hundred dollars down on the house. That leaves sixty-five hundred dollars. Monday morning I want you to take this money and take three thousand dollars and put it in a savings account for Beneatha's medical schooling. The rest you put in a checking account – with your name on it. And from now on any penny that come out of it or that go in it is for you to look after. For you to decide. (*She drops her hands a little helplessly.*) It ain't much, but it's all I got in the world and I'm putting in your hands. I'm telling you to be the head of this family from now on like you supposed to be.

Walter (*stares at the money*)   You trust me like that, Mama?

Mama   I ain't never stop trusting you. Like I ain't never stop loving you.

She goes out, and **Walter** *sits looking at the money on the table as the music continues in its idiom, pulsing in the room. Finally, in a decisive gesture, he gets up, and, in mingled joy and desperation, picks up the money. At the same moment,* **Travis** *enters for bed.*

Travis   What's the matter, Daddy? You drunk?

Walter (*sweetly, more sweetly than we have ever known him*)   No, Daddy ain't drunk. Daddy ain't going to never be drunk again . . .

Travis   Well, good night, Daddy.

Walter *has come from behind the couch and leans over, embracing his son.*

Walter   Son, I feel like talking to you tonight.

Travis   About what?

Walter   Oh, about a lot of things. About you and what kind of man you going to be when you grow up . . . Son . . . son, what do you want to be when you grow up?

Travis   A bus driver.

Walter (*laughing a little*)   A what? Man, that ain't nothing to want to be!

Travis   Why not?

Walter   'Cause, man – it ain't big enough – you know what I mean.

Travis   I don't know then. I can't make up my mind. Sometimes Mama asks me that too. And sometimes when I tell you I just want to be like you – she says she don't want me to be like that and sometimes she says she does . . .

Walter (*gathering him up in his arms*)   You know what, Travis? In seven years you going to be seventeen years old. And things is going to be very different with us in seven years. Travis . . . One day when you are seventeen I'll come home – home from my office downtown somewhere –

Travis   You don't work in no office, Daddy.

Walter   No – but after tonight. After what your daddy gonna do tonight, there's going to be offices – a whole lot of offices . . .

Travis   What you gonna do tonight, Daddy?

Walter   You wouldn't understand yet, son, but your daddy's gonna make a transaction . . . a business transaction that's going to change our lives . . . that's how come one day when you 'bout seventeen years old I'll come home and I'll be pretty tried, you know what I mean, after a day of conferences and secretaries getting things wrong the way they do . . . 'cause an executive's life is hell, man – (*The more* *he talks the further away he gets.*) And I'll pull the car up on the driveway . . . just a plain black Chrysler, I think with white walls – no – black tires. More elegant. Rich people don't have to be flashy . . . though I'll have to get something a little sportier for Ruth – maybe a Cadillac convertible to do her shopping in . . . And I'll come up the steps to the house and the gardener will be clipping away at the hedges and I'll say 'Hello, Jefferson how are you this evening?' And I'll go inside and Ruth will come downstairs and meet me at the door and we'll kiss each other, she'll take my arm and we'll go up to your room to see you sitting on the floor with the catalogues of all the great schools in America around you . . . All the great schools in the world! And – and I'll say, all right son – it's your seventeenth birthday, what is it you've decided? . . . Just tell me, what it is you want to be – and you'll be it . . . Whatever you want to be – Yessir! (*He holds his arms open for* **Travis**.) You just name it son . . . (**Travis** *leaps into them.*) and I hand you the world!

Walter*'s voice has risen in pitch and hysterical promise and on the last line he lifts* **Travis** *high.*

Curtain.

Scene Three

Saturday, moving day, one week later.

Before the curtain rises, **Ruth***'s voice, a strident, dramatic church alto, cuts through the silence.*

It is, in the darkness, a triumphant surge, a penetrating statement of expectation: 'Oh, Lord, I don't feel no ways tired! Children, oh, glory Hallelujah!'

As the curtain rises we see that **Ruth** *is alone in the living-room, finishing up the family's packing. It is moving day. She is nailing crates and tying cartons.* **Beneatha** *enters, carrying a guitar case, and watches her exuberant sister-in-law.*

Ruth Hey!

Beneatha (*putting away the case*)   Hi.

Ruth (*pointing at a package*)   Honey – look in that package there and see what I found on sale this morning at the South Centre. (**Ruth** *gets up and moves to the package and draws out some curtains.*) Lookahere – hand-turned hems!

Beneatha   How do you know the window size out there?

Ruth (*who hadn't thought of that*)   Oh – well, they bound to fit something in the whole house. Anyhow, they was too good a bargain to pass up. (**Ruth** *slaps her head, suddenly remembering something.*) Oh, Bennie – I meant to put a special note on that carton over there. That's your mama's good China and she wants 'em to be very careful with it.

Beneatha   I'll do it.

Beneatha *finds a piece of paper and starts to draw large letters on it.*

Ruth   You know what I'm going to do soon as I get in that new house?

Beneatha   What?

Ruth   Honey – I'm going to run me a tub of water up to here . . . (*With her fingers practically up to her nostrils.*) And I'm going to get in it – and I am going to sit . . . and sit . . . and sit in that hot water and the first person who knocks to tell *me* to hurry up and come out –

Beneatha   Gets shot at sunrise.

Ruth (*laughing happily*)   You said it, sister! (*Noticing how large* **Beneatha** *is absent-mindedly making the note.*) Honey, they ain't going to read that from no airplane.

Beneatha (*laughing to herself*)   I guess I always think things have more emphasis if they are big, somehow.

Ruth (*looking up at her and smiling*)   You and your brother seem to have that as a philosophy of life. Lord, that man –

done changed so 'round here. You know – you know what
we did last night? Me and Walter Lee?

Beneatha   What?

Ruth (*smiling to herself*)   We went to the movies. (*Looking at*
Beneatha *to see if she understands.*) We went to the movies.
You know the last time me and Walter went to the movies
together?

Beneatha   No.

Ruth   Me neither. That's how long it been. (*Smiling again.*)
But we went last night. The picture wasn't much good, but
that didn't seem to matter. We went – and we held hands.

Beneatha   Oh, Lord!

Ruth   We held hands – and you know what?

Beneatha   What?

Ruth   When we come out of the show it was late and dark
and all the stores and things was closed up . . . and it was
kind of chilly and there wasn't many people on the streets
. . . and we was still holding hands, me and Walter.

Beneatha   You're killing me.

Walter *enters with a large package. His happiness is deep in him; he
cannot keep still with his new-found exuberance. He is singing and
wiggling and snapping his fingers. He puts his package in a corner and
puts a record, which he has brought in with him, on the record player.
As the music comes up he dances over to* **Ruth** *and tries to get her to
dance with him. She gives in at last to his raunchiness and in a fit of
giggling allows herself to be drawn into his mood and together they
deliberately burlesque an old social dance of their youth.*

Beneatha (*regarding them a long time as they dance, then drawing
in her breath for a deeply exaggerated comment which she does not
particularly mean*)   Talk about – oldddddddddd-
fashionedddddddd – Negroes!

Walter (*stopping momentarily*)   What kind of Negroes?

He says this in fun. He is not angry with her today, nor with anyone. He starts to dance with his wife again.

Beneatha   Old-fashioned.

Walter (*as he dances with* **Ruth**)   You know, when these *New Negroes* have their convention – (*pointing at his sister*) – that is going to be the chairman of the Committee on Unending Agitation. (*He goes on dancing, then stops.*) Race, race, race! . . . Girl, I do believe you are the first person in the history of the entire human race to successfully brainwash yourself. (**Beneatha** *breaks up and he goes on dancing. He stops again, enjoying his tease.*) Damn, even the N double A C P takes a holiday sometimes! (**Beneatha** *and* **Ruth** *laugh. He dances some more with* **Ruth** *and starts to laugh and stops and pantomimes someone over an operating table.*) I can just see that chick someday looking down at some poor cat on an operating table before she starts to slice him, saying . . . (*pulling his sleeves back maliciously*) 'By the way, what are your views on civil rights down there? . . .'

He laughs at her again and starts to dance happily. The bell sounds.

Beneatha   Sticks and stones may break my bones but . . . words will never hurt me!

Beneatha *goes to the door and opens it as* **Walter** *and* **Ruth** *go on with the clowning.* **Beneatha** *is somewhat surprised to see a quiet good-looking middle-aged white man in a business suit holding his hat, a briefcase in his hand, and consulting a small piece of paper.*

Man   Uh – how do you do, miss. I am looking for a Mrs. (*he looks at the slip of paper*) Mrs. Lena Younger?

Beneatha (*smoothing her hair with slight embarrassment*)   Oh – yes, that's my mother. Excuse me. (*She closes the door and turns to quiet the other two.*) Ruth! Brother! Somebody's here. (*Then she opens the door. The man casts a curious quick glance at all of them.*) Uh – come in please.

Man (*coming in*)   Thank you.

Beneatha   My mother isn't here just now. Is it business?

Man   Yes . . . well, of a sort.

Walter (*freely, the Man of the House*)   Have a seat. I'm Mrs. Younger's son. I look after most of her business matters.

Ruth and **Beneatha** *exchange amused glances.*

Man (*regarding* **Walter**, *and sitting*)   Well – my name is Karl Lindner . . .

Walter (*stretching out his hand*)   Walter Younger. This is my wife – (**Ruth** *nods politely*) – and my sister.

Lindner   How do you do.

Walter (*amiably, as he sits himself easily on a chair, leaning forward on his knees with interest and looking expectantly into the newcomer's face*)   What can we do for you, Mr. Lindner?

Lindner (*some minor shuffling of the hat and briefcase on his knees*) Well – I am a representative of the Clybourne Park Improvement Association –

Walter (*pointing*)   Why don't you sit your things on the floor?

Lindner   Oh – yes. Thank you. (*He slides the briefcase and hat under the chair.*) And as I was saying – I am from the Clybourne Park Improvement Association and we have had it brought to our attention at the last meeting that you people – or at least your mother – has bought a piece of residential property at (*he digs for the slip of paper again*) four o six Clybourne Street . . .

Walter   That's right. Care for something to drink? Ruth, get Mr. Lindner a beer.

Lindner (*upset for some reason*)   Oh – no, really. I mean thank you very much, but no, thank you.

Ruth (*innocently*)   Some coffee?

Lindner   Thank you, nothing at all.

Beneatha *is watching the man carefully.*

Lindner   Well, I don't know how much you folks know about our organization. (*He is a gentle man; thoughtful and somewhat laboured in his manner.*) It is one of these community organizations set up to look after – oh, you know, things like block upkeep and special projects and we also have what we call our New Neighbours Orientation Committee . . .

Beneatha (*drily*)   Yes – and what do they do?

Lindner (*turning a little to her and then returning the main force to* **Walter**)   Well – it's what you might call a sort of welcoming committee, I guess. I mean they, we, I'm the chairman of the committee – go around and see the new people who move into the neighbourhood and sort of give them the lowdown on the way we do things out in Clybourne Park.

Beneatha (*with appreciation of the two meanings, which escape* **Ruth** *and* **Walter**)   Un-huh.

Lindner   And we also have the category of what the association calls – (*he looks elsewhere*) – uh – special community problems . . .

Beneatha   Yes – and what are some of those?

Walter   Girl, let the man talk.

Lindner (*with understated relief*)   Thank you. I would sort of like to explain this thing in my own way. I mean I want to explain to you in a certain way.

Walter   Go ahead.

Lindner   Yes. Well. I'm going to try to get right to the point. I'm sure we'll all appreciate that in the long run.

Beneatha   Yes.

Walter   Be still now!

Lindner   Well – ·

Ruth (*still innocently*)   Would you like another chair – you don't look comfortable.

Lindner (*more frustrated than annoyed*)   No, thank you very much. Please. Well – to get right to the point I – (*a great breath, and he is off at last*) I am sure you people must be aware of some of the incidents which have happened in various parts of the city when coloured people have moved into certain areas – (**Beneatha** *exhales heavily and starts tossing a piece of fruit up and down in the air.*) Well – because we have what I think is going to be a unique type of organization in American community life – not only do we deplore that kind of thing – but we are trying to do something about it. (**Beneatha** *stops tossing and turns with a new quizzical interest to the man.*) We feel – (*gaining confidence in this mission because of the interest in the faces of the people he is talking to*) – we feel that most of the trouble in this world, when you come right down to it – (*he hits his knee for emphasis*) – most of the trouble exists because people just don't sit down and talk to each other.

Ruth (*nodding as she might in church, pleased with the remark*) You can say that again, mister.

Lindner (*more encouraged by such affirmation*)   That we don't try hard enough in this world to understand the other fellow's problem. The other guy's point of view.

Ruth   Now that's right.

Beneatha *and* **Walter** *merely watch and listen with genuine interest.*

Lindner   Yes – that's the way we feel out in Clybourne Park. And that's why I was elected to come here this afternoon and talk to you people. Friendly like, you know, the way people should talk to each other and see if we couldn't find some way to work this thing out. As I say, the whole business is a matter of *caring* about the other fellow. Anybody can see that you are a nice family of folks, hard working and honest I'm sure. (**Beneatha** *frowns slightly, quizzically, her head tilted regarding him.*) Today everybody knows what it means to be on the outside of *something*. And of course, there is always somebody who is out to take the advantage of people who don't always understand.

Walter What do you mean?

Lindner Well – you see our community is made up of people who've worked hard as the dickens for years to build up that little community. They're not rich and fancy people; just hard-working, honest people who don't really have much but those little homes and a dream of the kind of community they want to raise their children in. Now, I don't say we are perfect and there is a lot wrong in some of the things they want. But you've got to admit that a man, right or wrong, has the right to want to have the neighbourhood he lives in a certain kind of way. And at the moment the overwhelming majority of our people out there feel that people get along better, take more of a common interest in the life of the community, when they share a common background. I want you to believe me when I tell you that race prejudice simply doesn't enter into it. It is a matter of the people of Clybourne Park believing, rightly or wrongly, as I say, that for the happiness of all concerned that our Negro families are happier when they live in their *own* communities.

Beneatha (*with a grand and bitter gesture*)   This, friends, is the Welcoming Committee!

Walter (*dumbfounded, looking at* **Lindner**)   Is this what you came marching all the way over here to tell us?

Lindner Well, now we've been having a fine conversation. I hope you'll hear me all the way through.

Walter (*tightly*)   Go ahead, man.

Lindner You see – in the face of all things I have said, we are prepared to make your family a very generous offer . . .

Beneatha Thirty pieces and not a coin less!

Walter Yeah?

Lindner (*putting on his glasses and drawing a form out of the briefcase*)   Our association is prepared, through the collective effort of our people, to buy the house from you at a financial gain to your family.

Ruth   Lord have mercy, ain't this the living gall!

Walter   All right, you through?

Lindner   Well, I want to give you the exact terms of the financial arrangement –

Walter   We don't want to hear no exact terms of no arrangements. I want to know if you got any more to tell us 'bout getting together?

Lindner (*taking off his glasses*)   Well – I don't suppose that you feel . . .

Walter   Never mind how I feel – you got any more to say 'bout how people ought to sit down and talk to each other? . . . Get out of my house, man.

He turns his back and walks to the door.

Lindner (*looking around at the hostile faces and, reaching and assembling his hat and briefcase*)   Well – I don't understand why you people are reacting this way. What do you think you are going to gain by moving into a neighbourhood where you just aren't wanted and where some elements – well – people can get awful worked up when they feel that their whole way of life and everything they've ever worked for is threatened.

Walter   Get out.

Lindner (*at the door, holding a small card*)   Well – I'm sorry it went like this.

Walter   Get out.

Lindner (*almost sadly regarding* **Walter**)   You just can't force people to change their hearts, son.

He turns and puts his card on a table and exits. **Walter** *pushes the door to with stinging hatred, and stands looking at it.* **Ruth** *just sits and* **Beneatha** *just stands. They say nothing.* **Mama** *and*

Travis *enter*.

Mama   Well – this all the packing got done since I left out of here this morning. I testify before God that my children got all the energy of the dead. What time the moving men due?

Beneatha   Four o'clock. You had a caller, Mama. (*She is smiling teasingly*.)

Mama   Sure enough – who?

Beneatha (*her arms folded saucily*)   The Welcoming Committee.

Walter *and* **Ruth** *giggle*.

Mama (*innocently*)   Who?

Beneatha   The Welcoming Committee. They said they're sure going to be glad to see you when you get there.

Walter (*devilishly*)   Yeah, they said they can't hardly wait to see your face.

Laughter.

Mama (*sensing their facetiousness*)   What's the matter with you all?

Walter   Ain't nothing the matter with us. We just telling you 'bout the gentleman who came to see you this afternoon. From the Clybourne Park Improvement Association.

Mama   What he want?

Ruth (*in the same moods as* **Beneatha** *and* **Walter**)   To welcome you, honey.

Walter   He said they can't hardly wait. He said the one thing they don't have, that they just *dying* to have out there is a fine family of coloured people! (*To* **Ruth** *and* **Beneatha.**) Ain't that right?

Ruth *and* **Beneatha** (*mockingly*)   Yeah! He left his card in case –

They indicate the card, and **Mama** *picks it up and throws it on the floor – understanding and looking off as she draws her chair up to the table on which she has put her plant and some sticks and some cord.*

Mama   Father, give us strength. (*Knowingly – and without fun*) Did he threaten us?

Beneatha   Oh – Mama – they don't do it like that any more. He talked Brotherhood. He said everybody ought learn how to sit down and hate each other with good Christian fellowship.

She and **Walter** *shake hands to ridicule the remark.*

Mama (*sadly*)   Lord, protect us –

Ruth   You should hear the money those folks raised to buy the house from us. All we paid and then some.

Beneatha   What they think we going to do – eat 'em?

Ruth   No, honey, marry 'em.

Mama (*shaking her head*)   Lord, Lord, Lord . . .

Ruth   Well – that's the way the crackers crumble. Joke.

Beneatha (*laughing noticing what her mother is doing*).   Mama, what are you doing?

Mama   Fixing my plant so it won't get hurt none on the way . . .

Beneatha   Mama, you going to take *that* to the new house?

Mama   Un-huh –

Beneatha   That raggedy-looking old thing?

Mama (*stopping and looking at her*)   It expresses *me*.

Ruth (*with delight, to* **Beneatha**)   So there, Miss Thing!

Walter *comes to* **Mama** *suddenly and bends down behind her and squeezes her in his arms with all his strength. She is overwhelmed by the suddenness of it and, though delighted, her manner is like that of* **Ruth** *with* **Travis**.

Mama   Look out now, boy! You make me mess up my thing here!

Walter (*his face lit, he slips down on his knees beside her, his arms still about her*)   Mama . . . you know what it means to climb up in the chariot?

Mama (*gruffly, very happy*)   Get on away from me now . . .

Ruth (*near the gift-wrapped package, trying to catch* **Walter**'s *eye*). Psst –

Walter   What the old song say, Mama . . .

Ruth   Walter – Now? (*She is pointing at the package.*)

Walter (*speaking the lines, sweetly, playfully, in his mother's face*)
   I got wings . . . you got wings . . .
   All God's children got wings . . .

Mama   Boy – get out of my face and do some work . . .

Walter
   When I get to heaven gonna put on my wings,
   Gonna fly all over God's heaven . . .

Beneatha (*teasingly, from across the room*)   Everybody talking 'bout heaven ain't going there!

Walter (*to* **Ruth**, *who is carrying the box across to them*)   I don't know, you think we ought to give her that . . . Seems to me she ain't been very appreciative around here.

Mama (*eyeing the box, which is obviously a gift*)   What is that?

Walter (*taking it from* **Ruth** *and putting it on the table in front of* **Mama**)   Well – what you all think. Should we give it to her?

Ruth   Oh – she was pretty good today.

Mama　I'll good you – (*She turns her eyes to the box again.*)

Beneatha　Open it, Mama.

She stands up, looks at it, turns and looks at all of them, and then presses her hands together and does not open the package.

Walter (*sweetly*)　Open it, Mama. It's for you. (**Mama** *looks in his eyes. It is the first present in her life without it being Christmas. Slowly she opens her package and lifts out, one by one, a brand-new sparkling set of gardening tools.* **Walter** *continues, prodding.*) Ruth made up the note – read it . . .

Mama (*picking up the card and adjusting her glasses*)　'To our own Mrs. Miniver – love from Brother, Ruth and Beneatha.' Ain't that lovely . . .

Travis (*tugging at his father's sleeve*)　Daddy, can I give her mine now?

Walter　All right, son. (**Travis** *flies to get his gift.*) Travis didn't want to go in with the rest of us, Mama. He got his own. (*Somewhat amused.*) We don't know what it is . . .

Travis (*racing back in the room with a large hatbox and putting it in front of his grandmother*)　Here!

Mama　Lord have mercy, baby. You done gone and bought your grandmother a hat?

Travis (*very proud*)　Open it!

She does and lifts out an elaborate, but very elaborate, wide gardening hat, and all the adults break up at the sight of it.

Ruth　Travis, honey, what is that?

Travis (*who thinks it is beautiful and appropriate*)　It's a gardening hat! Like the ladies always have on in the magazines when they work in their gardens.

Beneatha (*giggling fiercely*)　Travis – we were trying to make Mama Mrs. Miniver – not Scarlett O'Hara!

Mama (*indignantly*)   What's the matter with you all! This here is a beautiful hat! (*Absurdly*.) I always wanted me one just like it!

She pops it on her head to prove it to her grandson, and the hat is ludicrous and considerably oversized.

Ruth   Hot dog! Go, Mama!

Walter (*doubled over with laughter*)   I'm sorry, Mama – but you look like you ready to go out and chop you some cotton sure enough!

*They all laugh except **Mama**, out of deference to **Travis**'s feelings.*

Mama (*gathering the boy up to her*)   Bless your heart – this is the prettiest hat I ever owned – (**Walter**, **Ruth** and **Beneatha** *chime in – noisily, festively and insincerely congratulating* **Travis** *on his gift.*) What are we all standing around here for? We ain't finished packin' yet. Bennie, you ain't packed one book.

The bell rings.

Beneatha   That couldn't be the movers . . . it's not hardly two good yet –

Beneatha *goes into her room.* **Mama** *starts for the door.*

Walter (*turning, stiffening*)   Wait – wait – I'll get it. (*He stands and looks at the door.*)

Mama   You expecting company son?

Walter (*Just looking at the door*)   Yeah – yeah . . .

Mama *looks at* **Ruth**, *and they exchange innocent and unfrightened glances.*

Mama (*not understanding*)   Well, let them in, son.

Beneatha (*from her room*)   We need some more string.

Mama   Travis – you run to the hardware and get me some string cord.

Mama *goes out and* **Walter** *turns and looks at* **Ruth**. **Travis** *goes to a dish for money.*

Ruth Why don't you answer the door, man?

Walter (*suddenly bounding across the floor to her*) 'Cause sometimes it hard to let the future begin! (*Stooping down to her face.*)

    I got wings! You got wings!
    All God's children got wings!

He crosses to the door and throws it open. Standing there is a very slight little man in a not too prosperous business suit and with haunted frightened eyes and a hat pulled down tightly, brim up, around his forehead. **Travis** *passes between the men and goes out.* **Walter** *leans deep to the man's face, still in his jubilance.*

    When I get to heaven gonna put on my wings,
    Gonna fly all over God's heaven . . .

The little man just stares at him.

    Heaven –

(*Suddenly he stops and looks past the little man into the empty hallway.*) Where's Willy, man?

Bobo He ain't with me.

Walter (*not disturbed*) Oh – come on in. You know my wife.

Bobo (*dumbly, taking off his hat*) Yes – h'you, Miss Ruth.

Ruth (*quietly, a mood apart from her husband already, seeing* **Bobo**) Hello, Bobo.

Walter You right on time today . . . Right on time. That's the way! (*He slaps* **Bobo** *on his back.*) Sit down . . . lemme hear.

Ruth *stands stiffly behind them, as though somehow she senses death, her eyes fixed on her husband.*

Bobo (*his frightened eyes on the floor, his hat in his hands.*)   Could I please get a drink of water, before I tell you it, Walter Lee?

Walter *does not take his eyes off the man.* **Ruth** *goes blindly to the tap and gets a glass of water and brings it to* **Bobo**.

Walter   There ain't nothing wrong, is there?

Bobo   Lemme tell you –

Walter   Man – didn't nothing go wrong?

Bobo   Lemme tell you – Walter Lee. (*Looking at* **Ruth** *and talking to her more than* **Walter**)   You know how it was. I got to tell you how it was. I mean first I got to tell you how it was all the way . . . I mean about the money I put in, Walter Lee . . .

Walter   (*with taut agitation now*)   What about the money you put in?

Bobo   Well – is wasn't much as we told you – me and Willy – (*He stops.*) I'm sorry, Walter. I got a bad feeling about it. I got a real bad feeling about it . . .

Walter   Man, what you telling me about all this for? . . . Tell me what happened in Springfield . . .

Bobo   Springfield.

Ruth (*like a dead woman*)   What was supposed to happen in Springfield?

Bobo (*to her*)   This deal that me and Walter went into with Willy – Me and Willy was going to go down to Springfield and spread some money 'round so's we wouldn't have to wait so long for the liquor licence . . . That's what we were going to do. Everybody said that was the way you had to do, you understand, Miss Ruth?

Walter   Man – what happened down there?

Bobo (*a pitiful man, near tears*)   I'm trying to tell you, Walter.

Walter (*screaming at him suddenly*)   THEN TELL ME, GOD-DAMMIT . . . WHAT'S THE MATTER WITH YOU?

Bobo   Man . . . I didn't go to no Springfield, yesterday.

Walter (*halted, life hanging in the moment*)   Why not?

Bobo (*the long way, the hard way to tell*)   'Cause I didn't have no reasons to . . .

Walter   Man, what are you talking about?

Bobo   I'm talking about the fact that when I got to the train station yesterday morning – eight o'clock like we planned . . . Man – *Willy didn't never show up.*

Walter   Why . . . where was he . . . where is he?

Bobo   That's what I'm trying to tell you . . . I don't know . . . I waited six hours . . . I called his house . . . and I waited . . . six hours . . . I waited in that train station six hours . . . (*Breaking into tears.*) That was all the extra money I had in the world . . . (*Looking up at* **Walter** *with the tears running down his face.*) Man, *Willy is gone.*

Walter   Gone, what you mean Willy is gone? Gone where? You mean he went by himself. You mean he went off to Springfield by himself – to take care of getting the licence – (*Turns and looks anxiously at* **Ruth.**) You mean maybe he didn't want too many people in on the business down there? (*Looks to* **Ruth** *again, as before.*) You know Willy got his own ways. (*Looks back to* **Bobo.**) Maybe you was late yesterday and he just went on down there without you. Maybe – maybe – he's been callin' you at home tryin' to tell you what happened or something. Maybe – maybe – he just got sick. He's somewhere – he's got to be somewhere. We just got to find him – me and you got to find him. (*Grabs* **Bobo** *senselessly by the collar and starts to shake him.*) We got to!

Bobo (*in sudden angry, frightened agony*)   What's the matter with you, Walter! *When a cat take off with your money he don't leave no maps!*

Walter (*turning madly, as though he is looking for* **Willy** *in the very room*) Willy! . . . Willy . . . don't do it . . . Please don't do it . . . Man, not with that money . . . Man, please, not with that money . . . Oh, God . . . Don't let it be true . . . (*He is wandering around, crying out for Willy and looking for him or perhaps for help from God.*) Man . . . I trusted you . . . Man, I put my life in your hands . . . (*He starts to crumple down on the floor as* **Ruth** *just covers her face in horror.* **Mama** *opens the door and comes into the room, with* **Beneatha** *behind her.*) Man . . . (*He starts to pound the floor with his fists, sobbing wildly.*) That money is made out of my father's flesh . . .

Bobo (*standing over him helplessly*) I'm sorry, Walter . . . (*Only* **Walter***'s sobs reply.* **Bobo** *puts on his hat.*) I had my life staked on this deal, too . . .

He goes.

Mama (*to* **Walter**) Son – (*She goes to him, bends down to him, talks to his bent head.*) Son . . . Is it gone? Son, I gave you sixty-five hundred dollars. Is it gone? All of it? Beneatha's money too?

Walter (*lifting his head slowly*) Mama . . . I never . . . went to the bank at all . . .

Mama (*not wanting to believe him*) You mean . . . your sister's school money . . . you used that too . . . Walter? . . .

Walter Yesss! . . . All of it . . . It's all gone . . .

There is total silence. **Ruth** *stands with her face covered with her hands;* **Beneatha** *leans forlornly against a wall, fingering a piece of red ribbon from the mother's gift.* **Mama** *stops and looks at her son without recognition and then, quite without thinking about it, starts to beat him senselessly in the face.* **Beneatha** *goes to them and stops it.*

Beneatha Mama!

Mama *stops and looks at both her children and rises slowly and wanders vaguely, aimlessly away from them.*

Mama   I seen . . . him . . . night after night . . . come in
. . . and look at that rug . . . and then look at me . . . the red
showing in his eyes . . . the veins moving his head . . . I seen
him grow thin and old before he was forty . . . working and
working and working like somebody's old horse . . . killing
himself . . . and you – you give it all away in a day . . .

Beneatha   Mama –

Mama   Oh, God . . . (*She looks up to Him.*) Look down here
– and show me the strength.

Beneatha   Mama –

Mama (*folding over*)   Strength . . .

Beneatha (*plaintively*)   Mama . . .

Mama   Strength!

Curtain.

Act Three

An hour later.

At curtain, there is a sullen light of gloom in the living-room, grey light not unlike that which began the first scene of Act One. At left we can see **Walter** *within his room, alone with himself. He is stretched out on the bed, his shirt out and open, his arms under his head. He does not smoke, he does not cry out, he merely lies there, looking up at the ceiling, much as if he were alone in the world.*

In the living-room **Beneatha** *sits at the table, still surrounded by the now almost ominous packing crates. She sits looking off. We feel that this is a mood struck perhaps an hour before, and it lingers now, full of the empty sound of profound disappointment. We see on a line from her brother's bedroom the sameness of their attitudes. Presently the bell rings and* **Beneatha** *rises without ambition or interest in answering. It is* **Asagai**, *smiling broadly, striding into the room with energy and happy expectation and conversation.*

Asagai   I came over . . . I had some free time. I thought I might help with the packing. Ah, I like the look of packing crates! A household in preparation for a journey! It depresses some people . . . but for me . . . it is another feeling. Something full of the flow of life, do you understand? Movement, progress . . . It makes me think of Africa.

Beneatha   Africa!

Asagai   What kind of a mood is this? Have I told you how deeply you move me?

Beneatha   He gave away the money, Asagai . . .

Asagai   Who gave away what money?

Beneatha   The insurance money. My brother gave it away.

Asagai   Gave it away?

Beneatha   He made an investment! With a man even Travis wouldn't have trusted.

Asagai   And it's gone?

Beneatha   Gone!

Asagai   I'm very sorry . . . And you, now?

Beneatha   Me? . . . Me? . . . Me I'm nothing . . . Me. When I was very small . . . we used to take our sleds out in the wintertime and the only hills we had were the ice-covered stone steps of some houses down the street. And we used to fill them in with snow and make them smooth and slide down them all day . . . and it was very dangerous you know . . . far too steep . . . and sure enough one day a kid named Rufus came down too fast and hit the sidewalk . . . and we saw his face just split open right there in front of us . . . And I remember standing there looking at his bloody open face thinking that was the end of Rufus. But the ambulance came and they took him to the hospital and they fixed the broken bones and they sewed it all up . . . and the next time I saw Rufus he just had a little line down the middle of his face . . . I never got over that . . .

Walter *sits up, listening on the bed. Throughout this scene it is important that we feel his reaction at all times, that he visibly respond to the words of his sister and* **Asagai**

Asagai   What?

Beneatha   That that was what one person could do for another, fix him up – sew up the problem, make him alright again. That was the most marvellous thing in the world . . . I wanted to do that. I always thought it was the one concrete thing in the world that a human being could do. Fix up the sick, you know – and make them whole again. This was truly being God . . .

Asagai   You wanted to be God?

Beneatha   No – I wanted to cure. It used to be so important to me. I wanted to cure. It used to matter. I used to care. I mean about people and how their bodies hurt . . .

Asagai   And you've stopped caring?

Beneatha   Yes – I think so.

Asagai   Why?

Walter *rises, goes to the door of his room and is about to open it, then stops and stands listening, leaning on the door jamb.*

Beneatha   Because it doesn't seem deep enough, close enough to what ails mankind! It was a child's way of seeing things – or an idealist's.

Asagai   Children see all things very well sometimes – and idealists even better.

Beneatha   I know that's what you think. Because you are still where I left off. You with all your talk and dreams about Africa! You still think you can patch up the world. Cure the Great Sore of colonialism with the Penicillin of Independence –

Asagai   Yes!

Beneatha   Yes – 'Independence!' But then what? What about all the crooks and thieves and just plain idiots who will come into power and steal and plunder the same as before – only now they will be black and do it in the name of the new Independence – what about them?

Asagai   That will be the problem for another time. First we must get there.

Beneatha   And where does it end?

Asagai   End? Who even spoke of an end? To life? To living?

Beneatha   An end to misery! To stupidity! While I was sleeping in my bed things were happening in the world that directly concerned me – they just went out and did things –

and changed my life. Don't you see there isn't any real progress, Asagai, there is only one large circle that we march in, around and around each of us with our own little picture in front of us – our own little mirage that we think is the future.

Asagai   That is the mistake.

Beneatha   What?

Asagai   What you just said – about the circle. It isn't a circle – it is simply a long line – as in geometry, you know, one that reaches into infinity. And because we cannot see the end – we also cannot see how it changes. And it is very odd but those who see the changes, who dream, are called 'idealist' – and those who see only the circle we call them the 'realists'. It is very strange, and amusing too, I think.

Beneatha   You – you are almost religious.

Asagai   Yes . . . I think I have the religion of doing what is necessary in the world – and of worshipping man – because he is so marvellous, you see.

Beneatha   Man is foul! And the human race deserves its misery!

Asagai   You see you have become the religious one, in the old sense. Already, and after such a small defeat, you are worshipping despair.

Beneatha   From now on, I worship the truth – and the truth is that people are puny, small and selfish . . .

Asagai Truth? Why is it that you despairing ones always think that only you have the truth? I never thought to see *you* like that. You! Your brother made a stupid, childish mistake – and you are grateful to him. So that now you can give up the ailing human race on account of it. You talk about what good is struggle; what good is anything? Where are we all going? And why are we bothering?

Beneatha   *And you cannot answer it!*

Asagai (*shouting over her*)   *I live the answer!* (*Pause.*) In my village at home it is the exceptional man who can even read a newspaper . . . or who ever *sees* a book at all. I will go home and much of what I will have to say will seem strange to the people of my village . . . But I will teach and work and things will happen, slowly and swiftly. At times it will seem that nothing changes at all . . . and then again . . . the sudden dramatic events which make history leap into the future. And then quiet again. Retrogression even. Guns, murder, revolution. And I even will have moments when I wonder if the quiet was not better than all that death and hatred. But I will look about my village at the illiteracy and disease and ignorance and I will not wonder long. And perhaps . . . perhaps I will be a great man . . . I mean perhaps I will hold on to the substance of truth and find my way always with the right course . . . and perhaps for it I will be butchered in my bed some night by the servants of empire . . .

Beneatha   *The martyr!*

Asagai   . . . or perhaps I shall live to be a very old man respected and esteemed in my new nation . . . And perhaps I shall hold office and this is what I'm trying to tell you, Alaiyo; perhaps the things I believe now for my country will be wrong and outmoded, and I will not understand and do terrible things to have things my way or merely to keep my power. Don't you see that there will be young men and women, not British soldiers then, but my own black countrymen . . . to step out of the shadows some evening and slit my then useless throat? Don't you see they have always been there . . . that they always will be. And that such a thing as my own death will be an advance? They who might kill me even . . . actually replenish me!

Beneatha   Oh, Asagai, I know all that.

Asagai   Good! Then stop moaning and groaning and tell me what you plan to do.

Beneatha   Do?

Asagai   I have a bit of a suggestion.

Beneatha   What?

Asagai (*rather quietly for him*)   That when it is all over – that you come home with me –

Beneatha (*slapping herself on the forehead with exasperation born of misunderstanding*)   Oh – Asagai – at this moment you decide to be romantic!

Asagai (*quickly understanding the misunderstanding*)   My dear, young creature of the New World – I do not mean across the city – I mean across the ocean; home – to Africa.

Beneatha (*slowly understanding and turning to him with murmured amazement*)   To – to Nigeria?

Asagai   Yes! . . . (*Smiling and lifting his arms playfully.*) Three hundred years later the African Prince rose up out of the sees and swept the maiden back across the middle passage over which her ancestors had come –

Beneatha (*unable to play*)   Nigeria?

Asagai   Nigeria. Home. (*Coming to her with genuine romantic flippancy.*)   I will show you our mountains and our stars; and give you cool drinks from gourds and teach you the old songs and the way of our people – and, in time, we will pretend that (*very softly*) you have only been away for a day –

She turns her back to him, thinking. He swings her round and takes her full in his arms in a long embrace which proceeds to passion.

Beneatha (*pulling away*)   You're getting me all mixed up –

Asagai   Why?

Beneatha   Too many things – too many things have happened today. I must sit down and think. I don't know what I feel about anything right this minute.

She promptly sits down and props her chin on her fist.

Asagai (*charmed*)   All right, I shall leave you. No – don't get up. (*Touching her, gently, sweetly.*) Just sit awhile and think . . . Never be afraid to sit awhile and think. (*He goes to the door and looks at her.*) How often I have looked at you and said, 'Ah – so this is what the New World hath finally wrought . . .'

He goes. **Beneatha** *sits on alone. Presently* **Walter** *enters from his room and starts to rummage through things, feverishly looking for something. She looks up and turns in her seat.*

Beneatha (*hissingly*)   Yes – just look at what the New World hath wrought! . . . Just look! (*She gestures with bitter disgust.*) There he is! *Monsieur le petit bourgeois noir* – himself! There he is – Symbol of a Rising Class! Entrepreneur! Titan of the system! (**Walter** *ignores her completely and continues frantically and destructively looking for something and hurling things to the floor and tearing things out of their place in his search.* **Beneatha** *ignores the eccentricity of his actions and goes on with the monologue of insult.*) Did you dream of yachts on Lake Michigan, Brother? Did you see yourself on that Great Day sitting down at the Conference Table, surrounded by all the mighty bald-headed men in America? All halted, waiting, breathless, waiting for your pronouncements on industry? Waiting for you – Chairman of the Board? (**Walter** *finds what he is looking for – a small piece of white paper – and pushes it in his pocket and puts on his coat and rushes out without even having looked at her. She shouts after him.*) I look at you and I see the final triumph of stupidity in the world!

The door slams and she returns to just sitting again. **Ruth** *comes quickly out of* **Mama**'s *room.*

Ruth   Who was that?

Beneatha   Your husband.

Ruth Where did he go?

Beneatha   Who knows – maybe he has an appointment at U.S. Steel.

Ruth (*anxiously, with frightened eyes*)   You didn't say nothing bad to him, did you?

Beneatha   Bad? Say anything bad to him? No – I told him he was a sweet boy and full of dreams and everything is strictly peachy keen, as the ofay kids say!

Mama *enters from her bedroom. She is lost, vague, trying to catch hold, to make some sense of her former command of the world, but it still eludes her. A sense of waste overwhelms her gait; a measure of apology rides on her shoulders. She goes to her plant, which has remained on the table, looks at it, picks it up and takes it to the window sill and sits it outside, and she stands and looks at it a long moment. Then she closes the window, straightens her body with effort and turns round to her children.*

Mama   Well – ain't it a mess in here, though? (*A false cheerfulness, a beginning of something.*) I guess we all better stop moping around and get some work done. All this unpacking and everything we got to do. (**Ruth** *raises her head slowly in response to the sense of the line; and* **Beneatha** *in similar manner turns very slowly to look at her mother.*) One of you all better call the moving people and tell 'em not to come.

Ruth Tell 'em not to come?

Mama   Of course, baby. Ain't no need in 'em coming all the way here and having to go back. They charges for that too. (*She sits down, fingers her brow, thinking.*) Lord, ever since I was a little girl, I always remembers people saying, 'Lena – Lena Eggleston, you aims too high all the time. You needs to slow down and see life a little more like it is. Just slow down some.' That what they always used to say down home – 'Lord, that Lena Eggleston is a high-minded thing. She'll get her due one day!'

Ruth   No, Lena . . .

Mama   Me and Big Walter just didn't never learn right.

Ruth   Lena, no! We gotta go. Bennie – tell her . . . (*She rises and crosses to* **Beneatha** *with her arms outstretched.*

Beneatha *doesn't respond.*) Tell her we can still move . . . the notes ain't but a hundred and twenty five a month. We got four grown people in this house – we can work . . .

Mama (*to herself*)   Just aimed too high all the time –

Ruth (*turning and going to* **Mama** *fast – the words pouring out with urgency and desperation*)   Lena – I'll work . . . I'll work twenty hours a day in all the kitchens in Chicago . . . I'll strap my baby on my back if I have to and scrub all the floors in America and wash all the sheets in America if I have to – but we got to move . . . We got to get out of here . . .

Mama *reaches out absently and pats* **Ruth**'s *hand.*

Mama   No – I sees things differently now. Been thinking 'bout some of things we could do to fix this place up some. I seen a second-hand bureau over on Maxwell Street just the other day that could fit right there. (*She points to where the new furniture might go.* **Ruth** *wanders away from her.*) Would need some new handles on it and then a little varnish and then it look like something brand-new. And – we can put up them new curtains in the kitchen . . . Why this place be looking fine. Cheer us all up so that we forget trouble ever came . . . (*To* **Ruth.**) And you could get some nice screens to put up in your room round the baby's basinet . . . (*She looks at both of them, pleadingly.*) Sometimes you just got to know when to give up some things . . . and hold on to what you got.

Walter *enters from the outside, looking spent and leaning against the door, his coat hanging from him.*

Mama   Where you been, son?

Walter (*breathing hard*)   Made a call.

Mama   To who, son?

Walter   To The Man.

Mama   What man, baby?

Walter   The Man, Mama. Don't you know who The Man is?

Ruth   Walter Lee?

Walter   *The Man.* Like the guys in the streets says – The Man. Captain Boss – Mistuh Charley . . . Old Captain Please Mr. Bossman . . .

Beneatha (*suddenly*)   Lindner!

Walter   That's right! That's good. I told him to come right over.

Beneatha (*fiercely, understanding*)   For what? What do you want to see him for!

Walter (*looking at his sister*)   We going to do business with him.

Mama   What you talking 'bout, son?

Walter   Talking 'bout life, Mama. You all always telling me to see life like it is. Well – I laid in there on my back today . . . and I figure it out. Life just like it is. Who gets and who don't get. (*He sits down with his coat on and laughs.*) Mama, you know it's all divided up. Life is. Sure enough. Between the takers and the 'tooken'. (*He laughs.*) I've figured it out finally. (*He looks around at them.*) Yeah. Some of us always getting 'tooken'. (*He laughs.*) People like Willy Harris, they don't never get 'tooken'. And you know why the rest of us do? 'Cause we all mixed up. Mixed up bad. We get to looking 'round for the right and the wrong; and we worry about it and cry about it and stay up nights trying to figure out 'bout the wrong and right of things all the time . . . And all the time, man, them takers is out there operating, just taking and taking. Willy Harris? Shoot – Willy Harris don't even count. He don't even count in the big scheme of things. But I'll say one thing for old Willy Harris . . . he's taught me something. He's taught me to keep my eye on what counts in this world. Yeah – (*Shouting out a little.*) Thanks, Willy!

Ruth   What did you call that man for, Walter Lee?

Walter   Called him to tell him to come over to the show. Gonna put on a show for the man. Just what he wants to see. You see, Mama, the man came here today and he told us that them people out there where you want us to move – well they so upset they willing to pay us not to move out there. (*He laughs again.*) And – and, oh, Mama – you would have been proud of the way me and Ruth and Bennie acted. We told him to get out . . . Lord have mercy! We told the man to get out. Oh, we was some proud folks this afternoon, yeah. (*He lights a cigarette.*) We were still full of that old-time stuff . . .

Ruth (*coming towards him slowly.*)   You talking 'bout taking them people's money to keep us from moving in that house?

Walter   I ain't just talking 'bout it, baby – I'm telling you that's what's going to happen.

Beneatha   Oh, God! Where is the bottom! Where is the real honest-to-God bottom so he can't go any farther!

Walter   See – that's the old stuff. You and that boy that was here today. You all want everybody to carry a flag and a spear and sing some marching songs, huh? You wanna spend your life looking into things and trying to find the right and the wrong part, huh? Yeah. You know what's going to happen to that boy someday – he'll find himself sitting in a dungeon, locked in forever – and the takers will have the key! Forget it, baby! There ain't no causes – there ain't nothing but taking in this world, and he who takes most is smartest – and it don't make a damn bit of difference *how*.

Mama   You make something inside me cry, son. Some awful pain inside me.

Walter   Don't cry, Mama. Understand. That white man is going to walk in that door able to write cheques for more money than we ever had. It's important to him and I'm going to help him . . . I'm going to put on the show, Mama.

Mama   Son – I come from five generations of people who was slaves and sharecroppers – but ain't nobody in my family never let nobody pay 'em no money that was a way of telling us we wasn't fit to walk the earth. We ain't never been that poor. (*Raising her eyes and looking at him.*) We ain't never been that dead inside.

Beneatha   Well – we are dead now. All the talk about dreams and sunlight that goes on in this house. All dead.

Walter   What's the matter with you all! I didn't make this world! It was give to me this way! Hell, yes, I want me some yachts someday! Yes, I want to hang some real pearls 'round my wife's neck. Ain't she supposed to wear no pearls? Somebody tell me – tell me, who decides which women is suppose to wear pearls in this world. I tell you I am a *man* – and I think my wife should wear some pearls in this world!

This last line hangs a good while and **Walter** *begins to move about the room. The word 'man' has penetrated his consciousness; he mumbles it to himself repeatedly between strange agitated pauses as he moves about.*

Mama   Baby, how you going to feel on the inside?

Walter   Fine! . . . Going to feel fine . . . a man . . .

Mama   You won't have nothing left then, Walter Lee.

Walter (*coming to her*)   I'm going to feel fine, Mama. I'm going to look that son-of-a-bitch in the eyes and say – (*he falters*) – and say, 'All right, Mr. Lindner – (*he falters even more*) – that's your neighbourhood out there. You got the right to keep it like you want. You got the right to have it like you want. Just write the cheque and – the house is yours.' And, and I am going to say – (*his voice almost breaks*) And you – you people just put the money in my hand and you won't have to live next to this bunch of stinking niggers! . . . (*He straightens up and moves away from his mother, walking around the room.*) Maybe – maybe I'll just get down on my black knees . . . (*He does so;* **Ruth** *and* **Bennie** *and* **Mama** *watch him in frozen horror.*) Captain, Mistuh, Bossman. (*He starts crying.*) Ahee-hee-hee! (*Wringing his hands in profoundly anguished imitation.*) Yasssssuh! Great White Father, just gi' ussen de money, fo' God's sake, and we's ain't gwine come out deh and dirty up yo' white folks neighbourhood . . .

He breaks down completely, then gets up and goes into the bedroom.

Beneatha   That is not a man. That is nothing but a toothless rate.

Mama   Yes – death done come in this here house. (*She is nodding, slowly, reflectively.*) Done come walking in my house. On the lips of my children. You what supposed to be my beginning again. You – what supposed to be my harvest. (*To* **Beneatha**.) You – you mourning your brother?

Beneatha   He's no brother of mine.

Mama   What you say?

Beneatha   I said that that individual in that room is no brother of mine.

Mama   That's what I thought you said. You feeling like you better than he is today? (**Beneatha** *does not answer.*) Yes? What you tell him a minute ago? That he wasn't a man? Yes? You give him up for me? You done wrote his epitaph too – like the rest of the world? Well, who give you the privilege?

Beneatha   Be on my side for once! You saw what he just did, Mama! You saw him – down on his knees. Wasn't it you who taught me – to despise any man who would do that. Do what he's going to do.

Mama   Yes – I taught you that. Me and your daddy. But I thought I taught you something else too . . . I thought I taught you to love him.

Beneatha   Love him? There is nothing left to love.

Mama   There is always something left to love. And if you ain't learned that, you ain't learned nothing. (*Looking at her.*) Have you cried for that boy today? I don't mean for yourself

and for the family 'cause we lost the money. I mean for him;
what he been through and what it done to him. Child, when
do you think is the time to love somebody the most; when
they done good and made things easy for everybody? Well,
then, you ain't through learning – because that ain't the
time at all. It's when he's at his lowest and can't believe it
hisself 'cause the world done whipped him so. When you
starts measuring somebody, measure him right, child,
measure him right. Make sure you done taken into account
what hills and valleys he come through before he got to
wherever he is.

Travis *bursts into the room at the end of the speech, leaving the door
open.*

Travis   Grandmama – the moving men are downstairs!
The truck just pulled up.

Mama (*turning and looking at him*)   Are they, baby? They
downstairs?

She sighs and sits. **Lindner** *appears in the doorway. He peers in and
knocks lightly, to gain attention, and comes in. All turn to look at him.*

Lindner (*hat and briefcase in hand*)   Uh – hello . . .

Ruth *crosses mechanically to the bedroom door and opens it and lets it
swing open freely and slowly as the lights come up on* **Walter** *within,
still in his coat, sitting at the far corner of the room. He looks up and
out through the room to* **Lindner***.*

Ruth   He's here.

A long minute passes and **Walter** *slowly gets up.*

Lindner (*coming to the table with efficiency, putting his briefcase on
the table and starting to unfold papers and unscrew fountain pens.*)
Well, I certainly was glad to hear from you people. (**Walter**
*has begun to trek out of the room, slowly and awkwardly, rather like a
small boy, passing the back of his sleeve across his mouth from time to
time.*) Life can really be so much simpler than people let it be
most of the time. Well – with whom do I negotiate? You,
Mrs. Younger, or your son here? (**Mama** *sits with her hands*

folded on her lap and her eyes closed as **Walter** *advances.* **Travis**
goes close to **Lindner** *and looks at the paper curiously.*) Just some
official papers, sonny.

Ruth   Travis, you go downstairs.

Mama (*opening her eyes and looking into* **Walter***'s*)   No.
Travis, you stay right here. And you make him understand
what you doing, Walter Lee. You teach him good. Like
Willy Harris taught you. You show where our five
generations done come to. Go ahead, son –

Walter (*looks down into his boy's eyes.* **Travis** *grins at him merrily
and* **Walter** *draws him beside him with his arm lightly around his
shoulder.*)   Well, Mr. Lindner. (**Beneatha** *turns away.*) We
called you (*there is a profound, simple groping quality in his speech*)
because, well, me and my family . . . (*He looks around and shifts
from one foot to the other.*) Well – we are very plain people . . .

Lindner   Yes –

Walter   I mean – I have worked as a chauffeur most of
my life – and my wife here, she does domestic work in
people's kitchens. So does my mother. I mean – we are
plain people . . .

Lindner   Yes, Mr. Younger –

Walter (*really like a small boy, looking down at his shoes and then
up at the man*)   And – uh – well, my father, well, he was a
labourer most of his life.

Lindner (*absolutely confused*)   Uh, yes –

Walter (*looking down at his toes once again*)   My father almost
beat a man to death once because this man called him a bad
name or something, you know what I mean?

Lindner   No, I'm afraid I don't.

Walter (*finally straightening up*)   Well, what I mean is that
we come from people who had a lot of pride. I mean – we
are very proud people. And that's my sister over there and
she's going to be a doctor – and we are very proud –

Lindner   Well – I am sure that is very nice, but –

Walter (*starting to cry and facing the man eye to eye*)   What I am telling you is that we called you over here to tell you that we are very proud and that this is – this is my son, who makes the sixth generation of our family in this country, and that we have all thought about your offer and we have decided to move into our house because my father – my father – he earned it. (**Mama** *has her eyes closed and is rocking back and forth as though she were in church, with her head nodding the amen yes.*) We don't want to make no trouble for nobody or fight no causes – but we will try to be good neighbours. That's all we got to say. (*He looks the man absolutely in the eyes.*) We don't want your money. (*He turns and walks away from the man.*)

Lindner (*looking around at all of them*)   I take it then that you have decided to occupy.

Beneatha   That's what the man said.

Lindner (*to* **Mama** *in her reverie*)   Then I would like to appeal to you, Mrs. Younger. You are older and wiser and understand things better I am sure . . .

Mama (*rising*)   I am afraid you don't understand. My son said we was going to move and there ain't nothing left for me to say. (*Shaking her head with double meaning*) You know how these young folks is nowadays, mister. Can't do a thing with 'em. Good-bye.

Lindner (*folding up his materials*)   Well – if you are that final about it . . . There is nothing left for me to say. (*He finishes. He is almost ignored by the family, who are concentrating on* **Walter Lee**. *At the door* **Lindner** *halts and looks around.*) I sure hope you people know what you're doing. (*He shakes his head and goes.*)

Ruth (*looking around and coming life*)   Well, for God's sake – if the moving men are here – LET'S GET THE HELL OUT OF HERE!

Mama (*into action*)   Ain't it the truth! Look at all this here mess. Ruth put Travis's good jacket on him . . . Walter Lee, fix your tie and tuck your shirt in, you look just like somebody's hoodlum. Lord have mercy, where is my plant? (*She flies to get it amid the general bustling of the family, who are deliberately trying to ignore the nobility of the past moment.*) You all start on down . . . Travis child, don't go empty-handed . . . Ruth, where did I put that box with my skillets in it? I want to be in charge of it myself . . . I'm going to make us the biggest dinner we ever ate tonight . . . Beneatha, what's the matter with them stockings? Pull them things up, girl . . .

The family starts to file out as two moving men appear and begin to carry out the heavier pieces of furniture, bumping into the family as they move about.

Beneatha   Mama, Asagai – asked me to marry him today and go to Africa –

Mama (*in the middle of her getting-ready activity*)   He did? You ain't old enough to marry nobody. (*See the moving men lifting one of her chairs precariously.*) Darling, that ain't no bale of cotton, please handle it so we can sit in it again. I had that chair twenty-five years . . .

The movers sigh with exasperation and go on with their work.

Beneatha (*girlishly and unreasonably trying to pursue the conversation*)   To go to Africa, Mama – be a doctor in Africa . . .

Mama (*distracted*)   Yes, baby –

Walter   Africa! What he want you to go to Africa for?

Beneatha   To practise there . . .

Walter   Girl, if you don't get all them silly ideas out your head! You better marry yourself a man with some loot . . .

Beneatha (*angrily, precisely as in the first scene of the play*) What have you got to do with who I marry?

Walter   Plenty. Now I think George Murchison –

He and **Beneatha** *go out yelling at each other vigorously;* **Beneatha** *is heard saying that she would not marry* **George Murchison** *if he were Adam and she were Eve, etc. The anger is loud and real till their voices diminish.* **Ruth** *stands at the door and turns to* **Mama** *and smiles knowingly.*

Mama (*fixing her hat at last*)   Yeah – they something all right, my children . . .

Ruth   Yeah – they're something. Let's go, Lena.

Mama (*stalling, starting to look around the house*)   Yes – I'm coming. Ruth –

Ruth   Yes?

Mama (*quietly, woman to woman*)   He finally come into his manhood today, didn't he? Kind of like a rainbow after the rain . . .

Ruth (*biting her lip lest her own pride explode in front of* **Mama**) Yes, Lena.

Walter*'s voice calls for them raucously.*

Mama (*waving* **Ruth** *out vaguely*)   All right, honey – go on down. I be down directly.

Ruth *hesitates, then goes.* **Mama** *stands at last alone in the living-room, her plant on the table before her as the lights start to come down. She looks around at all the walls and ceilings and suddenly, despite herself, while the children call below, a great heaving thing rises in her and she puts her fist to her mouth, takes a final desperate look, pulls her coat about her, pats her hat and goes out. The lights dim down. The door opens and she comes back in, grabs her plant, and goes out for the last time.*

Curtain.